Making the List

❦

Making the List

cx

A Cultural History
of the American Bestseller

1900–1999

cx

as seen through the annual bestseller lists
of Publishers Weekly

Michael Korda

BARNES
&NOBLE
BOOKS
NEW YORK

The author and publisher gratefully acknowledge the following sources of copyrighted material:

Material from *#1 New York Times Best Seller* by John Bear.
Copyright © 1992 by John Bear.
Reprinted with the permission of Ten Speed Press, Berkeley, CA.

Lyrics from "American Pie," reprinted by kind permission of Don McLean,
pub. Benny Bird Co. Inc, adm. Universal Songs.

Publishers Weekly bestseller lists, copyright © *Publishers Weekly*
reprinted with the permission of *Publishers Weekly*.

This edition published by Barnes & Noble Publishing, Inc.,
a division of Barnes & Noble, Inc., 122 Fifth Avenue, NY, NY 10011

2001 Barnes & Noble Books

Book design by Midori Nakamura

ISBN 0-7607-2559-4

Library of Congress Cataloging-in-Publication Data

Korda, Michael, 1933-
    Making the list : a cultural history of the American bestseller, 1900-1999 / Michael Korda.
        p.cm.
    Includes index.
    ISBN 0-7607-2559-4 (alk. paper)
        1. Best sellers—United States—Bibliography. 2. Books and reading—United States—
    History—20th century. 3. Popular literature—United States—History and criticism.
    I. Title.

    Z1033.B3 K67 2001
    381'.45002'0973—dc21

                                                                                    2001046473

Printed and bound in the United States of America

01 02 03 04 05 06 M 9 8 7 6 5 4 3 2 1

FG

Publisher's Note

Publishers Weekly compiled its first nonfiction list in
1912 to complement *The Bookman* fiction list. Since
1913, *Publishers Weekly* has compiled annual fiction and
nonfiction lists, with the exception of the years 1914–16,
for which no nonfiction lists were compiled.

The publisher would like to express its appreciation to
the staff of *Publishers Weekly* for their help with this book.
In particular, we would like to thank Daisy Maryles,
PW's Executive Editor.

TABLE OF CONTENTS

❧

INTRODUCTION

❧

T HE BESTSELLER LIST is such a part of our lives that it's hard to imagine how the book business, let alone authors, readers, and booksellers, could get along without it.

Of course it's a mixed blessing, in the eyes of most social and literary critics, since the bestseller list in their view tends to favor popular "story-tellers" over more "literary" novelists, celebrities over the unknown, "repeat" authors who write a book every year or so over those who write more slowly or those whose first book has just been published, people with trendy medical, sociological, or self-improvement schemes over writers who have spent a lifetime studying more "serious" subjects, brazen self-promoters over the shy, awkward, or physically unprepossessing, and so on.

All this is true up to a point, on the face of things. Certainly anybody packing a book bag for a long trip, as I have just done, with the intention of putting in some serious reading time, is unlikely to limit himself to the most recent big bestsellers, and most of us have favorite writers whose books never once appeared on the bestseller list. (Just so there are no secrets between us, my book bag contained the four large paperback volumes of Anthony Powell's *Dance to the Music of Time*; volume 3 of *The Churchill War Papers,* edited by Martin Gilbert; Barbara Kingsolver's *The Poisonwood Bible,* a big bestseller; about half a dozen novels by James Lee Burke in paperback; and a guide to Cairo, Alexandria, and the Nile.)

Nevertheless, as we shall see, a snobbish or elitist attitude toward the bestseller list is as unjustified as a slavish devotion to it. Many of the books I enjoy most have been big bestsellers in their time, including, for example, Larry McMurtry's *Lonesome Dove,* which is, along with Evelyn Waugh's *Brideshead Revisited* (also a bestseller), one of the books I often reread. Not every book on the bestseller list is exploitive, or trashy, or propelled there by Oprah. When one looks over the bestseller lists of the past hundred years, it is amazing how many good books are there, and how many of them have survived over the decades. Of course there are also a good many clunkers, fad diet books that have long since been made obsolete by new fad diets, "as told to" autobiographies by celebrities whose luster has grown dim, and so on, but that's the point—the bestseller list, from day one, has always represented a reliable mixture of the good and the bad, of quality and trash, of literature for the ages and self-improvement schemes that now seem merely weird to the extent they're remembered at all. (Who still remembers Dr. Coué or "primal scream therapy" or "winning through intimidation"? Is there anybody out there still taking safflower seed oil capsules to lose weight, as recommended in *Calories Don't Count?*)

The bestseller list, in fact, presents us with a kind of corrective reality. It tells us what we're *actually* reading (or, at least, what we're actually *buying*) as opposed to what we think we *ought* to be reading, or would like other people to believe we're buying. Like stepping on the scales, it tells us the truth, however unflattering, and is therefore, taken over the long haul, a pretty good way of assessing our culture and of judging how, if any, we have changed.

A word about me is in order. Having been an editor at Simon & Schuster for forty-three years, the bestseller list is part of my life, but not in a scholarly way. I look at it every week in much the same spirit that investors look at the list of stock prices, with a mixture of self-congratulation and self-loathing. (Well, we sure showed them with that book! How on earth did I miss buying *that* one?) It's the barometer of what is actually selling (and making money) in my trade, so I pay a certain amount of attention to it, naturally enough, in much the same way that a wheat farmer might follow wheat prices. On the other hand, I'm also an author, of thirteen books—five novels and eight works of nonfiction. My second book, *Power!,* was a #1 bestseller; my second novel, *Queenie,* went to #2 on the hardcover list and #1 on the paperback list. I mention all this only to make it clear that I am not just an *observer* of the bestseller list. I know what it feels like when a book you've published gets on the list, and I also know what it feels like when a book you've *written* gets on the list and even goes to #1. Perhaps equally important, I know what it feels like when your book falls off the list or doesn't make it there in the first place.

In short, we're not just talking numbers here, we're talking about people's lives, their ambitions, their success or failure. This isn't just literary history, it's a look at who we are, seen through what we read. People writing cookbooks (and books on nutrition) are fond of quoting the cliché, "You are what you eat" (actually a paraphrase of Ludwig Feuerbach's *"Der Mensch ist, was er isst"*—Man is what he eats), but true as that may be, it's also undeniable that you are what you *read,* that, as a nation and a society, the books we read, from decade to decade, tell us something about ourselves, where we've been, who we are, where we're going.

This is a project that inevitably involves a certain amount of nostalgia on my part, and on the part of anybody who has enjoyed reading over the years. Certain books will make us wish we could have the pleasure of reading them again for the first time; others will bring back fond memories, no doubt; still others may make us question our sanity, or at least that of the American reading public.

In general, I think, we are likely to be reminded again and again of Alphonse Karr's comment, *"Plus ça change, plus c'est la même chose"* (The more things change, the more they are the same). In every decade, from 1900 to the end of the twentieth century, people have been reliably attracted to the same kinds of books. If that were not the case, neither publishers nor booksellers could ever have made a living. Certain kinds of popular fiction always do well, as do diet books (a major staple of the trade, which also tells us something about American eating habits and American prosperity), self-help books, celebrity memoirs, sensationalist scientific or religious speculation, stories about pets, medical advice (particularly on the subjects of sex, longevity, and child rearing), folksy wisdom and/or humor, and the American Civil War.

An old publishing story relates that when Bennett Cerf, the cofounder of Random House, was asked to come up with the title for a book that was certain to be a major bestseller, he is said to have replied, *"Lincoln's Doctor's Dog,"* but Cerf had surely borrowed the line, since publishers were telling each other this one way back when he was still in knickers, the point being that there were certain neural bumps in the consciousness of the American reading public that, when combined and triggered off, would inevitably produce a bestseller—Civil War + doctor + dog = $, as it were—and all experience has proved this formula to be correct.

(Though, interestingly enough, when a book called *Lincoln's Doctor's Dog* finally *was* published, in 1939, it didn't do much, but then it was a spoof of sorts, so it may not count. The renowned bookman Christopher Morley wrote a story under that title, too, though Professor Merrill Peterson, the Lincoln scholar, remarked that it was "not a very good story.")

On the other hand, the bestseller list is full of surprises, too. Publishers have always bemoaned the fate of the dreaded "first novel," but the bestseller lists are full of first novels by unknown authors that sold hundreds of thousands of copies—even millions of copies—and made their author, and publisher, rich and famous; Margaret Mitchell's *Gone With the Wind* is the example that comes to everybody's mind. Lest anybody suppose that this doesn't happen anymore, let me mention the magic name Harry Potter. In much the same spirit, literary critics have always bemoaned the fact that serious literary fiction, particularly by first novelists, doesn't sell, but the bestseller lists often feature novels that sold tons of copies and were awarded literary prizes or good reviews (to name only two recent examples, Charles Frazier's *Cold Mountain* and Jeffrey Lent's *In the Fall*).

Of course, today, people complain that the bestseller list has become institutionalized, transformed into a kind of cultural tyranny that concentrates all the energy of publishers and booksellers into the service of the top bestsellers, whatever they may be, with no attention left over for the rest. There is some truth to this, of course, particularly in a culture like ours, that divides everyone and everything into winners and losers, but on the other hand, a real-life visit to a bookseller should be enough to dispel most of the fears people have on this score. Small- to medium-size independent bookstores are usually chockablock with books that have clearly been ordered according to the often eccentric whim or taste of the owner; as for the big national chains, their mall stores and superstores carry an incredibly wide variety of books, ranging far beyond the big bestsellers of the present or even the past. Of course the top bestsellers are placed up front where they can be easily seen and found—merchants have been doing that since the beginning of time—but a bookstore is likely to carry thousands of titles, only a small percentage of which will have been bestsellers. Indeed my first reaction on entering a bookstore is to stand there awed by the sheer diversity of human taste and interest; there is always a part of me wondering, "Who on earth would buy *that,* and why?"

Mind you, I have much the same reaction in looking through the catalogs of new books from my fellow publishers, and even through our own. Who on earth is going to read *that?* I ask myself over and over again at the description of yet another involuted, self-searching first novel or quirky nonfiction book or weirdly special cookbook. But that's the point. Ours is an industry defiantly determined to answer the needs of everybody who can read, however special, strange, or odd their taste and interests may be. We cling to the notion that somebody out there, God knows who, will buy that next French-Thai vegetarian fusion cookbook, this illustrated history of the world's battleships, that definitive biography of Lord Acton (yes, yes, "Power corrupts, and absolute power corrupts absolutely," but what *else* do you know about him, or *need* to know about him?), and so on.

The publishing legend Robert Gottlieb, back in the days when he was an editor at Simon & Schuster, once held an informal contest among his colleagues in the train on the way to the American Booksellers' Association convention in Washington, D.C., for the most boring title anybody could imagine for a book that might reasonably be published. The winner was *Canada, Friendly Giant to the North,* a joke that lost some of its savor the next day when somebody actually found a book by that title on display at another publisher's booth.

It was once said of President Lyndon B. Johnson that if he had owned a shoe store all the shoes in the store would have been in his own size, but publishers and booksellers go as far as they can in the other direction: They try to provide something for everyone. Who has ever entered a bookstore without seeing *something* they wanted to buy, something that catches the eye and about which one can say—albeit with a certain hesitation perhaps—"I've always wanted to read about that."

The bestseller list is therefore neither as predictable nor as dominating as its critics make it out to be. Plenty of really strange books get onto the list and stay there for a long time, and as much as booksellers may pay attention to the list, they still fill their stores with books that aren't on it. Despite the inherent suspicion on the part of authors that the list is manipulated by somebody, in fact it isn't controlled by publishers any more than it is by bookstores. Of course many of the books on it are reasonably predictable—particularly novels by big, established authors—but at least half of the books on any given week's bestseller list are there to the immense surprise and puzzlement of their publishers. That's why publishers find it so hard to repeat their successes— half the time they can't figure out how they happened in the first place. For that matter, authors have even been known to make their way onto the national bestseller lists *without* a publisher. Wayne Dyer, one of the self-help gurus of the 1970s, sold his first book, *Your Erroneous Zones,* from store to store across the country out of the back of his station wagon and was already high on the list before book publishers even noticed what was happening. The late Peter McWilliams, one of the early popularizers of Transcendental Meditation, did the same. In a sense, therefore, the list is democratic and does represent, very roughly, what people are interested in at a given moment in time, as opposed to only what people are trying to sell them.

There are lists of everything these days, not just books. The bestseller list started a trend, which has spread to just about everything that can be sold or merchandized. The top movies are listed by gross and sometimes by attendance; top records ditto; the top-selling cars are listed; celebrities and models are listed and rated by scores of magazines ("The Top Ten Blondes!" "The Top Ten Divorce Lawyers in New York!" "The Top Ten Hostesses in Washington!," etc.). We score everything and everyone, but when the top ten books were first listed by sales in 1895, it was a startling innovation in retailing, though it did not immediately catch on. (For those who are interested, the list for the year 1895 included, at #9, Anthony Hope's *The Prisoner of Zenda*, Israel Zangwill's *The Master,* and George du Maurier's *Trilby.* Zangwill is mostly remembered, if at all, as something of a cultural icon among early Zionists; *The Prisoner of Zenda* and *Trilby,* however, are still in print and can be read with great pleasure; in fact, it wouldn't be hard to imagine either one of them on the bestseller list today. The #1 book was *Beside the Bonnie Briar Bush,* by Ian Maclaren, which seems to have sunk without a trace at some point in the last 107 years, although it was also made into a successful play. *Sic transit gloria mundi.*)

As the late Alice Payne Hackett, an indefatigable lifetime student of the bestseller list, points out in her book, *70 Years of Best Sellers,* the most critical factor involved in creating a bestseller list was the passage of the international copyright law in 1891. Until that time, to put it bluntly, American publishers tended to "pirate" the works of successful English and European writers—that is, to republish them over here without the author's permission and above all without paying royalties—and far from wanting to draw attention to what they were publishing, they were more inclined to keep quiet about it. (Pirating books still goes on, though these days it is mostly in the other direction: American bestsellers are pirated in Taiwan, for sale throughout the Far East.) Prior to the passage of the copyright law, American publishers were wary of boasting about how many copies they had sold of a book, for fear the author might turn up and demand his or her money, but once copyright protection was instituted and the author's right to receive royalties was recognized, boasting about sales very quickly became a way of boosting sales, and the way was open for the bestseller list to be born.

Ms. Hackett, who had very firm opinions about everything concerned with books and who, as an editor of the book industry's trade journal *Publishers Weekly,* was in part responsible for drawing up the *PW* list every week for many years, attributes the invention to Harry Thurston Peck, a reviewer, and later editor, of the literary magazine *The Bookman,* which first began to run a monthly list of "best sellers" in 1895.

By 1902, the "best seller list" was firmly established and consisted at first of six books. The books featured on the list were determined by calling the major bookstores in several large cities, which is pretty much the way it is done today, give or take some new technology in the shape of computers.

If Peck was in fact the man who started it all, it should be noted that he did *not,* right from the beginning, ask book publishers what was selling, figuring, quite rightly that any book publisher would merely take that as an opportunity to boost his own wares. That, too, has not changed with time. It is still the number of copies actually *sold* ("out the door," as we say in the trade) that matters, not the number of copies shipped to the stores or the number printed. Ask a book publisher how many copies a book has sold, and he or she, presuming you're not the author, will probably try to remember the size of the first printing, then double it. If you're the author, the publisher will try to remember the number of copies that were shipped and cut that in half in order to avoid encouraging you to expect a big royalty check. Say what you will about bookselling, you can at least look at the pile of copies on a given table and tell whether it's grown smaller during the course of the day, and Peck was shrewd enough to know it.

In any case, there it is—I have it in my hands—the very first bestseller list (monthly at the time), from the February issue of *The Bookman: A Literary Journal,* along with a whole bunch of articles that look as if they could appear (unread) in the *New York Times Book Review* today. Curiously enough, the list is more detailed and chatty than it is today, with far more effort to break it down by region. On the other hand, nothing on it would be likely to surprise a book buyer or a book publisher 107 years later. *The Prisoner of Zenda* probably sells a lot of copies today (and was made into a movie for the umpteenth time only a few years ago), and the fact that Mrs. Herrick's *The Chafing Dish Supper* hit the list in Chicago wouldn't raise an eyebrow, either—it sounds like exactly the kind of quick, home-entertaining cookbook that still sells well a century later.

George Du Maurier's *Trilby* seems to have been what we would call a real national bestseller, #1 in Chicago; New York City; Albany, N.Y.; Cincinnati, Ohio; Indianapolis, Ind.; Kansas City, Mo.; St. Paul, Minn.; Rochester, N.Y.; Toledo, Ohio; Portland, Ore.; Portland, Maine; and Washington, D.C. Perhaps understandably, *Kentucky Cardinal* was #1 in Louisville, Ky.—regional best-sellers were already a phenomenon—and *Trilby* failed to make the list altogether in Boston, perhaps because it was considered too racy.

Ms. Hackett got it exactly right in pointing to the international make-up of the list. It was far more cosmopolitan than today's, and in the area of fiction, at any rate, still dominated by British or, to a lesser degree, European writers: George Du Maurier, Anthony Hope, Sir Arthur Conan Doyle, Walter Besant, etc. Still, that would change in time, as America became the dominant culture post–World War Two, and it is now relatively rare for a foreign author to hit the bestseller list, while in the rest of the world, particularly France—where resentment against American cultural imperialism extends beyond Coca-Cola, fast-food outlets, popular music, and the movies to books—intellectuals complain bitterly about the way their bestseller lists are increasingly dominated by American writers.

Interestingly enough, the March issue of *The Bookman,* with the *second* bestseller list, mentions the effect of weather on book sales for the first time, attributing lighter sales to severe snowstorms over most of the Midwest and Northeast, and also points to the importance of Valentine's Day and Easter for booksellers. *A Year of Paper Dolls* did well as a Valentine's Day present, for example, and probably wouldn't do badly today. Otherwise, *Trilby* continues to dominate the list.

(Ms. Hackett, by the way, also did authors an invaluable service by breaking bestsellers down into successful categories by subject, so if you're about to put this book down to get back to your word processor and are wondering what to write, you might want to keep in mind that in the category of "Crime and Suspense," Mickey Spillane's *I, the Jury* [1962] has sold over 6 million copies; that Dr. Spock's *Baby and Child Care* [1946] sold over 23 million copies; that among "Religious Novels," Charles Monroe Sheldon's *In His Steps* [1897] sold over 8 million copies; and that among "Westerns," Zane Grey topped the list for many years at over 2 million with his 1928 novel *Nevada.* Those who suppose that poetry is dead, at least in terms of sales, should bear in mind that *101 Famous Poems,* compiled by R. J. Cook [1916], has sold over 6 million copies, about the same (moving to the category of "Juveniles") as Frank Baum's *The Wizard of Oz* [1900], and almost three times the number of Gene Stratton Porter's *The Girl of the Limberlost* [1909]. Of course Ms. Hackett's figures were carefully compiled three decades ago, and for some of these books they may be even higher now, but it just goes to show how much it matters to pick the right category or subject when you sit down to write that book.)

The intimate electronic connection between the bestseller list, bookstores, publishers, and the media that now flourishes did not of course exist at the time, but from the very beginning the idea of listing books by the number of copies they sold in a given period seemed so right that it was hard to imagine what the book trade was like before its invention. As early as 1896, one year after the first bestseller list appeared, certain trends that are still with us today became apparent. William Jennings Bryan's unsuccessful campaign for the presidency (his trademark was his speech on the evils of the gold standard, a real stem-winder that ended with the famous peroration, "Thou shalt not crucify mankind upon a cross of gold!") made a bestseller out of *Coin's Financial School,* which attempted to explain for the layman the thorny subjects of bimetallism and the gold standard, thus beginning the long run of books about financial matters on the bestseller list and making the connection between politics and bestsellers; and the *Aeronautical Annual* hit the list in Boston, thus signifying the trend of new developments in science and technology to spur interest among book buyers. Another interesting fact was that Ian Maclaren had *two* novels on the 1896 list. *Beside the Bonnie Briar Bush* was still on the list a year after its appearance on the first list, and had been joined there by Maclaren's *Kate Carnegie,* thus making him the first of that select group of novelists whose books spend more than a year on the list, and of the even more select group with more than one title on the list at the same time. That books of real quality and literary value could hit the list was demonstrated once and for all by the appearance there of Stephen Crane's *The Red Badge of Courage,* a classic that continues to sell today. On the other hand, some bestselling authors like Mark Twain never hit the list, because he sold many of his books himself through subscription companies (the earliest form of book club) and house-to-house sales.

Once the bestseller list had appeared in its first form, it did not exactly take the world by storm. *Publishers Weekly,* the industry weekly magazine, moved quickly to adopt a list of its own, though it did not start including non-fiction books in its list until much later, and the *New York Times Book Review* did not get around to publishing its own bestseller list as a regular, weekly feature until 1942, while the *Wall Street Journal* did not get around to it until 1994, just ninety-nine years after the invention of the whole thing.

Part of the problem lay, no doubt, in the historic reluctance of book reviewers and the book review media to get embroiled in the sordid question of what is selling as opposed to the question of what is worth reading. From the very beginning, serious reviewers were dismayed with the bestseller list, and the marked tendency it demonstrated of Americans failing to heed the advice and warnings of book reviewers (then as now). Even today, a reader of the *New York Times Book Review* can hardly fail to note the obvious difference between the books that are prominently and/or seriously reviewed, and those that appear on the list, and there was certainly an initial reluctance, undiminished by time, to "rank" books by their sales, instead of by their merit.

On the whole, the honesty of the bestseller list, wherever it appears, has seldom been criticized. From time to time complaints are heard that movie companies and individuals try to influence the list by buying copies in bulk. Certainly this has been tried—movie producers have occasionally budgeted large amounts of money and sent their underlings out to buy up books at key bookstores that are known to report their sales to the *New York Times,* but the difficulty of this strategy is that you have to buy all those books at retail and then what do you do with them? I have been told of certain novels, made into big movies, that have been stacked up in storage areas in movie studios, and it may be so, but not too many people—not even that many movie companies—really want to buy fifty or a hundred thousand copies of a book just to get it onto the bestseller list. Whenever a movie producer or executive has suggested this procedure to me, I've found that they were under the impression that buying fifty or a hundred copies here and ten to twenty copies there would make a difference— when I've explained that nothing less than a well-planned (and well-financed) campaign of buying in bulk all across the country would really do the trick, they've always dropped the matter. Really, the list has been relatively scandal free, except for the occasion when William Peter Blatty, the author of *The Exorcist,* sued the *New York Times,* accusing them of deliberately keeping his novel *Legion* off the list, and lost his appeal in the U.S. Supreme Court. That was in 1983, and so far as I know there has been no scandal or legal problem since then.

Those interested in the minutiae of the list should run, not walk, to read John Bear's *The #1 New York Times Best Seller* (Ten Speed Press, 1992), which is certainly full of interesting facts (or "factoids," as my son Christopher calls recondite or useless information that you don't need to know). Bear's book will remind some readers of the famous publishing story about Alfred A. Knopf, who sent a little girl he knew a copy of a Knopf book about penguins, of which he was quite proud, and got back a letter that read:

"Dear Mr. Knopf, Thank you very much for the book, which told me more about penguins than I wanted to know."

I am gratified to know that I am in the book for *Power!* ("First #1 book by a top executive of a publishing house and only the second #1 title with an exclamation point"), but puzzled to know what to make of the following:

- ❖ "Only book by a Finnish author to become #1:
  The Egyptian by Mika Waltari in 1949."

- ❖ "Just over 2% of all #1 authors have accounted for more than 14% of all #1 best sellers."

- ❖ "First #1 best seller to be banned in Boston: *Strange Fruit* by Lillian Smith."

- ❖ "First book by a black man to reach #1: *Black Boy* by Richard Wright (Harper) in 1944."

- ❖ "Top 5 authors who reached #1 before they were 35:
  Françoise Sagan, *Bonjour Tristesse*, age 19.9
  Amy Wallace, *The Book of Lists*, 22
  Marion Hargrove, *See Here, Private Hargrove*, 23
  Bill Maudlin, *Up Front*, 23.8
  Norman Mailer, *The Naked and the Dead*, 25.4."

(Connoisseurs of factoids will be further interested to know that Ms. Wallace is the daughter of bestselling novelist Irving Wallace, one of only five authors to be #1 in fiction *and* nonfiction on the *New York Times* bestseller list.)

Obviously, there is a wealth of strange facts and coincidences in the bestseller list, but the most important thing is that it demonstrates the continuing interest of the American public in books and reading, despite the ever-growing competition from other, newer media. Up until World War Two, the only threat to the book industry was the movie business. After

World War Two, the book industry had to contend with television, too, and it was widely predicted that TV would kill the book. This did not happen. The invention of the home video player did not kill the book, nor did cable and satellite television, nor has the DVD player, nor even the home computer and the Internet. Despite these many, and increasingly high-tech, ways of spending leisure time, the book has survived and people continue to buy the big bestsellers. Possibly literacy itself is doomed in some kind of digitalized future, but for the moment, all we can say is that people are reading about as much as they ever did, that the big bestsellers are measured in numbers significantly higher than ever before, and that the bestseller list, in one form or another, is very likely to be with us, for better or for worse, for another hundred years more.

Critic and editor Roger Burlingame summed it up in 1947 about as well as it could be put:

> Certain themes are sure-fire for a lot of people. A sizeable following is guaranteed for a novel with a religious background. Books on success, self-improvement, the techniques of a popular game can be counted on. Mysteries have a special public. Certain authors have their own bodies of disciples. Someone once said that "an author is likely to be successful if he writes the same book over and over again." But what makes a book spread over all the groups and classes is a known but inexpressible secret.
>
> We can say that the public taste has widened immeasurably in the last fifty years. Many of the old bars are down. The public will accept realism. Tragedy, every aspect of life. Snobbery or squeamishness are gone. But it will accept sound romance too. It is probably safe to say that a good book has, today, a better chance of being a best seller than ever in American history.

That must have sounded optimistic in 1947 (two years before *The Egyptian* was #1), as people began to sit in front of that new presence in their living room, the soon to become ubiquitous television set, but it remains true, and in some ways it could have been written today. "Sound romance" still hits the list, as do realism and tragedy, and books on success and self-improvement. It would be difficult to agree that snobbery and squeamish-ness have gone—Burlingame may have been optimistic there—but writers who become great successes by writing the same book over and over again are certainly still with us, many of them right up there at the top of the list, week after week.

As we look at the bestsellers of the past hundred years, decade by decade, we will, perhaps, get a sense of just what it is that makes Americans buy a book in large quantities, of that elusive and mysterious mix of elements and appeal that makes a book, fiction or nonfiction, a bestseller. Burlingame, no dummy, denied there was a surefire formula, and he was right. Certain factors publishers can predict, but not the exact way in which they are combined to produce, suddenly, against all expectations, and out of the blue—a bestseller! Editors cling to the advice that's always worked for them, when dealing with authors—"Concentrate on story, story, story!" "*Show*, don't tell!" or, in the case of nonfiction, "Tell the reader what you're going to tell him, then tell him, then tell him what you've told him!"

Among other beliefs is that you have to grab the reader by the throat with the very first line of the book, that the central figure has to be sympathetic, that the story must end on a note of hope, but almost anybody can think of any number of bestselling novels that don't follow these specs. The lines that people remember from Dickens aren't usually the first lines in his novels, but occur later on; none of the brothers Karamazov is particularly sympathetic; Camus's novels end on a note of despair. Everybody at Simon & Schuster who read the manuscript of Larry McMurtry's *Lonesome Dove*, except me, thought it was a big mistake to kill off Gus toward the end of the book, but the novel went on to win the Pulitzer Prize and become a huge bestseller. Most people who read McMurtry's *Streets of Laredo,* the sequel to *Lonesome Dove,* thought it was a mistake to kill off Newt at the beginning of the book, but it, too, was a big bestseller.

The lesson is, yes, there *are* rules, but they don't apply to writers of real talent, and they're not absolute for anybody. The only thing you can say for sure is that, yes, the ability to tell a story matters a lot, in fiction and in non-fiction, and having something new and interesting to say about familiar subjects is maybe at the heart of it all.

Of course, as most readers will know, there is, strictly speaking, no one "bestseller list." Publishers tend to focus on the *New York Times Book Review* list, first of all because it's national, secondly because the imprimatur of the *Times* lends a certain weight to it, and finally because most book publishers live or work in New York City, and therefore regard the *Times* as their home-town paper as well as the paper of record on almost every subject. Not a few authors actually get a bonus for every week their book is on the *TBR* list, the amount varying from author to author, and usually rising as the book climbs the list. On the other hand, every major newspaper, and many magazines, has its own list, and naturally these reflect regional differences—a book can be on the *TBR* list week after week, but never appear at all, for example, on the *Los Angeles Times* list, and vice versa. The *Washington Post* bestseller list is heavily skewed toward nonfiction and political books, as you might suppose, and the *Los Angeles Times* list toward show business and celebrity books.

Usually, the top five books in fiction and nonfiction are the same all over the country, with minor variations in placing, and since the *New York Times* list is (supposedly) carefully balanced to represent national sales, it is usually accepted as representing the national sale of a book accurately, and probably does. The *New York Times* gets its information from key booksellers, just as Harry Thurston Peck did in 1895, and tries to keep a balance between small "independent" bookstores and the big bookstore chains like Barnes & Noble. Of course the bookstores each have their own bestseller lists, which sometimes differ radically from that of the *Times*.

Within the trade, the *Publishers Weekly* list has long been regarded by some as more accurate than the *Times,* and it is certainly more venerable, having begun in 1912. It is therefore the *PW* list—and Alice Payne Hackett's research on the bestseller list from 1895 to 1912, in her book *70 Years of Best Sellers*—that will be presented here, with the twentieth century divided into decades, which seems the sensible way to approach what would otherwise very likely be an indigestible mass of information.

To some degree, however, this arrangement, while convenient, is fictitious, for in fact the century needs to be divided into periods of cultural development, i.e., from 1900 to America's entry into the First World War in 1917, from the postwar period to the Crash of 1929 (or perhaps the subsequent election of Franklin Delano Roosevelt to the presidency in 1932), from 1941 to 1945 (the Second World War), then perhaps from 1946 to the assassination of John F. Kennedy in 1963, and from there to the end of the century.

Others might argue for different periods (or headings), but, as we shall no doubt see, America's cultural history, to the extent that it is represented by bestselling books, is naturally divided by the great events and changes of the century rather than by decades. Thus the rural, bucolic, and relatively innocent United States of the period from 1900 to 1917 confronts war and emerges into the "jazz age" and the wild times and flamboyant prosperity of the twenties, followed by the political and cultural shock of the Crash, the stern determination of the New Deal, then Pearl Harbor and World War Two, then the postwar period, with its curious combination of conformism concealing the beginning of huge societal changes, these two trends—conformity and rebellious change—coming to a head during the Vietnam War, then the long, slow birth of a whole new America whose culture and economy, spurred on by the collapse of Communism, would, for better or worse, come to dominate the world by the end of the century.

I have deliberately refrained from drawing any major conclusions in advance about what we will find in looking at the books Americans read from decade to decade throughout the previous century, in the hope that it will be a joint discovery, for me and for the reader. For those who are old enough, it will no doubt recall many pleasures and not a few embarrassments. For those who are younger, it may be instructive to realize what their parents or grandparents read, and to reflect, perhaps, on how few big bestsellers are remembered even a decade or so later, and on how quickly ideas, celebrities, and self-improvement schemes, however successfully merchandized, become old-fashioned, quaint, and yesterday's news.

Here, then, is a century of bestsellers.

CHAPTER ONE

1900–1909

☙

THE FIRST THING that strikes one about the bestseller lists for the years 1900 through 1909 that follow is the huge popularity of historical fiction, together with the relative decline of foreign and British authors. America was at last producing her own popular fiction, for better or for worse.

Some confusion has been created by the constant appearance of Winston Churchill on the bestseller list (in 1900, 1901, 1904, 1906, and 1908), but this prolific writer of (mostly) Southern historical fiction was not, in fact, the future prime minister of Great Britain, who would later write an unsuccessful novel himself as well as a ton of hugely successful works of history and autobiography.

Not much survives on current bookshelves from 1900, although #5 for the year, Irving Bacheller's *Eben Holden,* was famous in its day for picturing rural life in a somewhat idealistic form, and Charles Major's *When Knighthood Was in Flower* would be read for many years and was the prototype for many similar works of fiction up to and including a recent novel by Michael Crichton.

Both Irving Bacheller and Winston Churchill were back on the list with new books in 1901, so the current trend of bestselling authors coming out with a new book every year is nothing new. Those in the book publishing world who hesitate to bring out first novels by unknown authors should bear in mind that Bertha Runkle's first novel, *The Helmet of Navarre,* had an unprecedented first printing of 100,000 (the equivalent of at least half a million today) in 1901 and rose to #3 on the year's list.

The #1 bestseller of 1901 was Winston Churchill's *The Crisis,* perhaps the first big Civil War historical novel, establishing a new category that would culminate in *Gone With the Wind* and has still not exhausted itself— though we should bear in mind that in 1901 there were still plenty of people alive who remembered the war, or who had fought in it, since it had only ended thirty-six years before.

1902 brought a couple of memorable books, including A. Conan Doyle's *The Hound of the Baskervilles,* still today one of his most famous Sherlock Holmes novels, and the first "detective story," so far as I know, to make the list, as well as *Mrs. Wiggs of the Cabbage Patch,* by Alice Caldwell Hegan, which is still in print, and, at #1, Owen Wister's *The Virginian,* which was much later made into a hugely successful, indeed landmark motion picture, starring the young Gary Cooper.

1903 brought the English novelist Mrs. Humphry Ward to the top of the list for the year, with *Lady Rose's Daughter,* the first of many bestsellers by Mrs. Ward, who was the Danielle Steel of her day. *The Virginian* and *Mrs. Wiggs of the Cabbage Patch* were both still on the list a year later, but more striking is one of the first big "business novels" to make the list, *Letters of a Self-Made Merchant to His Son,* by George Horace Lorimer, establishing yet another enduring category in American publishing, leading to such huge modern-day bestsellers as Sloan Wilson's *The Man in the Gray Flannel Suit* (1955) and several of Ayn Rand's novels.

1904 saw the publication of an enduring American favorite, still read today, *Rebecca of Sunnybrook Farm,* by Kate Douglas Wiggin, while 1905 not only saw the publication of Edith Wharton's *The House of Mirth,* introducing on the list a major name in American fiction, but also the publication of *The Clansman,* by Thomas Dixon Jr., which D. W. Griffith made into the ur-American motion picture *The Birth of a Nation,* thus beginning, among other things, the movie business's practice of buying the rights to popular bestselling fiction as the basis for films.

Edith Wharton's novel was still on the bestseller list a year later, in 1906, together with yet another new novel at #1 from the apparently indefatigable Winston Churchill, but in terms of American literature, 1906 is chiefly famous for the publication of Upton Sinclair's *The Jungle,* a book that was not only enormously influential—Sinclair's unsparingly realistic portrayal of the meat-packing business played a large part in getting the Pure Food and Drug Act passed—but started the trend for bestselling novels that took on or "exposed" a big contemporary "subject," a trend that was to lead Sinclair himself to fame and fortune as a writer and was to start one of the major categories of successful fiction publishing, peaking perhaps with Irving Wallace in the 1960s, with his bestselling fictional exposés of the Kinsey Report, the Nobel Prize, etc., Arthur Hailey's *Hotel,* and Henry Morton Robinson's *The Water of Life.*

Alice Payne Hackett points out that in 1908 nine out of ten authors on the year's bestseller list were American (including John Fox Jr., whose *The Trail of the Lonesome Pine* would remain on the list for two years), and that 1909 marked the first *American* detective story to appear on the list, *The Man in Lower Ten,* by Mary Roberts Rinehart, thus beginning yet another successful fiction category, which thrives today in the hands of Mary Higgins Clark, and also inaugurating a long tradition of women novelists who use three names appearing on the bestseller list.

Of course the lists for these years are somewhat deceptive, in that non-fiction books aren't, as yet, included; still, what we see here gives some idea of what people who went to bookstores, as opposed to buying books by subscription or on a door-to-door basis (the early equivalents of the book club), never mind those who were still content to sit at home reading the family Bible, were buying and reading in quantity.

The America they represent is at once familiar and totally foreign. We must keep in mind that the automobile is still a rarity, about to be mass-produced for the first time; that roads, consequently, are mostly dirt, for the convenience of horses; that while the telegraph exists, of course, the telephone is still a rarity; that aviation is in its experimental infancy; that radio is as yet unthought of; that most people continue to live in the country, as opposed to the city; and that suburbs, shopping malls, the shirt with an attached collar, and supermarkets have yet to be even imagined.

It is a country that remains at heart simple and innocent and that still takes its ideas about culture, literature, art, and philosophy from Europe, which is at once admired for its civilization and deeply mistrusted for its deep class distinctions, and, especially in the case of France, its lack of moral high purpose. Much as we may now admire Theodore Roosevelt, anybody who reads his letters and speeches today can hardly fail to be struck by unflagging emphasis on America's presumed moral superiority, and it is therefore hardly surprising that the best-selling novels of the period have, by and large, a quaint innocence of tone. In the first decade of the twentieth century there were still plenty of people who regarded the reading of popular fiction not only as a waste of time, but as a sin, or at least as a way station on the road to sin, and the subject of sex in fiction was firmly *taboo,* and could, at best, only be hinted at. Both the novels of Tolstoy and Maupassant were widely criticized for dealing with forbidden subjects (adultery, for example, in *Anna Karenina*), and therefore "unwholesome." No doubt Americans were having the usual amount of sex, judging from the swiftly rising birthrate, but they certainly weren't *reading* about it. A whole host of official and unofficial censors assured the purity of the book, both at the local level, from the pulpit (in the days when the pulpit still mattered), and by the self-imposed caution of authors, publishers, and booksellers, who knew, or thought they knew, just how far book buyers were willing to go when reading fiction. The books on the bestseller lists for the years 1900 through 1909 are, therefore, on the whole, a pretty wholesome lot, but that is not to say that they don't fit into categories that would become fairly well established over the next fifty or sixty years, and are recognizable even today. First of all, there are historical novels, which proportionally take up far more of the list than they do today, but aren't really very different in tone—it will be several decades (and two world wars) before *Forever Amber* and *Mandingo* add graphic sex to the age-old recipe for successful historical fiction. Then, there are what we would now call "romantic novels"—one suspects that *To Have and to Hold,* by Mary Johnston (1900), could probably still be published successfully today, albeit with a different title. Finally, there are "subject" novels like *The Jungle* that are written to shock as well as to provide a lot of information and opinion in the guise of a novel, a genre that is still with us today, plus the odd "serious," that is to say, literary, bestseller, which then, as now, hit the list through some lucky combination of good reviews, clever publicity, and snob appeal, and the occasional "Western," at a time when the cowboy was still a living presence in the West, and the Battle of the Little Big Horn had occurred only twenty-five years earlier.

Book chains, like the mall stores and "superstores" as we know them today, hardly existed. The average American bookstore was small, independent, privately owned, and run by its owner, who bought books either directly from the publisher, with the help of regular visits from the publishers' "sales reps" (traveling salesmen who sold their employer's "list" of books) or through jobbers, the "middle men" of the book publishing industry. Since books were not commonly returnable, bookstores were cautious about the number of copies they ordered of any title, hence the amazement over the 100,000-copy first printing of Bertha Runkle's *The Helmet of Navarre.*

In small towns, the local bookshop was the center of cultural life, along with the library, of course. The book club had yet to be invented, although the "lending library" already existed in big cities, particularly for mysteries. The price of a book—$1.50 was about average—seems cheap to us, but it has to be remembered that in most small towns fifty cents or less would buy you a drugstore lunch, and that $1.50 was a meaningful amount of money for the average working man or woman, certainly enough to place books among the luxuries of middle-class life. The idea of discounting books had not, perhaps happily, occurred to anyone yet, though in big cities second-hand bookstores did a thriving business, and there were whole areas devoted to them.

Given the pace of events at the beginning of the century—the Russo-Japanese War, the growing tension in Europe between the monarchies of Russia, Austro-Hungary, and Germany, the huge growth of big cities, big industry (both targets of Upton Sinclair's novels), and high finance—the fiction on the best-seller lists for the decade seems decidedly tame and even escapist. "Genteel" and "proper," in fact, may be the words that first come to mind, and there is no doubt some truth to this, but then again, there is Upton Sinclair furiously blowing the lid off the scandalous and poisonous conditions in the meatpacking industry and making a bestseller of it, and there is Thomas Dixon Jr. writing about the Ku Klux Klan, albeit, we may think, on the wrong side of the issue, so the fiction market wasn't entirely hearts and flowers, though one may be forgiven for supposing that most of these books were read by women, with the possible exceptions of *The Jungle, The Clansman,* and *The Hound of the Baskervilles.*

Still this wasn't an age when men were supposed to sit around reading novels, or advertised the fact if they did so. President Roosevelt himself was an avid reader (and writer) of muscular nonfiction, and after attempting to read Tolstoy, had some harsh things to say about the great Russian novelist's immoral views on life and love, and this tendency certainly shows up in the books that made the list in the era before America's entry into the First World War radically changed her culture and her sense of self and produced a very different kind of bestseller list.

1900

FICTION

1. *To Have and to Hold*, by Mary Johnston. Houghton Mifflin

2. *Red Pottage*, by Mary Cholmondeley. Harper

3. *Unleavened Bread*, by Robert Grant. Scribner

4. *The Reign of Law*, by James Lane Allen. Macmillan

5. *Eben Holden*, by Irving Bacheller. Lothrop

6. *Janice Meredith*, by Paul Leicester Ford. Dodd, Mead

7. *The Redemption of David Corson*, by Charles Frederic Goss. Bowen-Merrill

8. *Richard Carvel*, by Winston Churchill. Macmillan

9. *When Knighthood Was in Flower*, by Charles Major. Bowen-Merrill

10. *Alice of Old Vincennes*, by Maurice Thompson. Bowen-Merrill

1901

FICTION

1. *The Crisis*, by Winston Churchill. Macmillan

2. *Alice of Old Vincennes*, by Maurice Thompson. Bowen-Merrill

3. *The Helmet of Navarre*, by Bertha Runkle. Century

4. *The Right of Way*, by Gilbert Parker. Harper

5. *Eben Holden*, by Irving Bacheller. Lothrop

6. *The Visits of Elizabeth*, by Elinor Glyn. John Lane

7. *The Puppet Crown*, by Harold MacGrath. Bowen-Merrill

8. *Richard Yea-and-Nay*, by Maurice Hewlett. Macmillan

9. *Graustark*, by George Barr McCutcheon. Stone & Kimball

10. *D'ri and I*, by Irving Bacheller. Lothrop

1902

FICTION

1. *The Virginian,* by Owen Wister. Macmillan

2. *Mrs. Wiggs of the Cabbage Patch,* by Alice Caldwell Hegan. Century

3. *Dorothy Vernon of Haddon Hall,* by Charles Major. Macmillan

4. *The Mississippi Bubble,* by Emerson Hough. Bowen-Merrill

5. *Audrey,* by Mary Johnston. Houghton Mifflin

6. *The Right of Way,* by Gilbert Parker. Harper

7. *The Hound of the Baskervilles,* by A. Conan Doyle. McClure, Phillips

8. *The Two Vanrevels,* by Booth Tarkington. McClure, Phillips

9. *The Blue Flower,* by Henry van Dyke. Scribner

10. *Sir Richard Calmady,* by Lucas Malet. Dodd, Mead

1903

FICTION

1. *Lady Rose's Daughter,* by Mrs. Humphry Ward. Harper

2. *Gordon Keith,* by Thomas Nelson Page. Scribner

3. *The Pit,* by Frank Norris. Doubleday, Page

4. *Lovey Mary,* by Alice Hegan Rice. Century

5. *The Virginian,* by Owen Wister. Macmillan

6. *Mrs. Wiggs of the Cabbage Patch,* by Alice Hegan Rice. Century

7. *The Mettle of the Pasture,* by James Lane Allen. Macmillan

8. *Letters of a Self-Made Merchant to His Son,* by George Horace Lorimer. Small, Maynard

9. *The One Woman,* by Thomas Dixon Jr. Doubleday, Page

10. *The Little Shepherd of Kingdom Come,* by John Fox Jr. Scribner

1904

FICTION

1. *The Crossing,* by Winston Churchill. Macmillan

2. *The Deliverance,* by Ellen Glasgow. Doubleday, Page

3. *The Masquerader,* Anonymous (Katherine Cecil Thurston). Harper

4. *In the Bishop's Carriage,* by Miriam Michelson. Bobbs-Merrill

5. *Sir Mortimer,* by Mary Johnston. Harper

6. *Beverly of Graustark,* by George Barr McCutcheon. Dodd, Mead

7. *The Little Shepherd of Kingdom Come,* by John Fox Jr. Scribner

8. *Rebecca of Sunnybrook Farm,* by Kate Douglas Wiggin. Houghton Mifflin

9. *My Friend Prospero,* by Henry Harland. McClure, Phillips

10. *The Silent Places,* by Stewart Edward White. McClure, Phillips

1905

FICTION

1. *The Marriage of William Ashe,* by Mrs. Humphry Ward. Harper

2. *Sandy,* by Alice Hegan Rice. Century

3. *The Garden of Allah,* by Robert Hichens. Stokes

4. *The Clansman,* by Thomas Dixon Jr. Doubleday, Page

5. *Nedra,* by George Barr McCutcheon. Dodd, Mead

6. *The Gambler,* by Katherine Cecil Thurston. Harper

7. *The Masquerader,* Anonymous (Katherine Cecil Thurston). Harper

8. *The House of Mirth,* by Edith Wharton. Scribner

9. *The Princess Passes,* by C. N. and A. M. Williamson. Holt

10. *Rose o' the River,* by Kate Douglas Wiggin. Houghton Mifflin

1906

FICTION

1. *Coniston,* by Winston Churchill. Macmillan

2. *Lady Baltimore,* by Owen Wister. Macmillan

3. *The Fighting Chance,* by Robert W. Chambers. Appleton

4. *The House of a Thousand Candles,* by Meredith Nicholson. Bobbs-Merrill

5. *Jane Cable,* by George Barr McCutcheon. Dodd, Mead

6. *The Jungle,* by Upton Sinclair. Doubleday, Page

7. *The Awakening of Helena Ritchie,* by Margaret Deland. Harper

8. *The Spoilers,* by Rex Beach. Harper

9. *The House of Mirth,* by Edith Wharton. Scribner

10. *The Wheel of Life,* by Ellen Glasgow. Doubleday, Page

1907

FICTION

1. *The Lady of the Decoration,* by Frances Little. Century

2. *The Weavers,* by Gilbert Parker. Harper

3. *The Port of Missing Men,* by Meredith Nicholson. Bobbs-Merrill

4. *The Shuttle,* by Frances Hodgson Burnett. Stokes

5. *The Brass Bowl,* by Louis J. Vance. Bobbs-Merrill

6. *Satan Sanderson,* by Hallie Erminíe Rives. Bobbs-Merrill

7. *The Daughter of Anderson Crow,* by George Barr McCutcheon. Dodd, Mead

8. *The Younger Set,* by Robert W. Chambers. Appleton

9. *The Doctor,* by Ralph Connor. Revell

10. *Half a Rogue,* by Harold MacGrath. Bobbs-Merrill

1908

FICTION

1. *Mr. Crewe's Career,* by Winston Churchill. Macmillan

2. *The Barrier,* by Rex Beach. Harper

3. *The Trail of the Lonesome Pine,* by John Fox Jr. Scribner

4. *The Lure of the Mask,* by Harold MacGrath. Bobbs-Merrill

5. *The Shuttle,* by Frances Hodgson Burnett. Stokes

6. *Peter,* by F. Hopkinson Smith. Scribner

7. *Lewis Rand,* by Mary Johnston. Houghton Mifflin

8. *The Black Bag,* by Louis J. Vance. Bobbs-Merrill

9. *The Man from Brodney's,* by George Barr McCutcheon. Dodd, Mead

10. *The Weavers,* by Gilbert Parker. Harper

1909

FICTION

1. *The Inner Shrine,* Anonymous (Basil King). Harper

2. *Katrine,* by Elinor Macartney Lane. Harper

3. *The Silver Horde,* by Rex Beach. Harper

4. *The Man in Lower Ten,* by Mary Roberts Rinehart. Bobbs-Merrill

5. *The Trail of the Lonesome Pine,* by John Fox Jr. Scribner

6. *Truxton King,* by George Barr McCutcheon. Dodd, Mead

7. *54-40 or Fight,* by Emerson Hough. Bobbs-Merrill

8. *The Goose Girl,* by Harold MacGrath. Bobbs-Merrill

9. *Peter,* by F. Hopkinson Smith. Scribner

10. *Septimus,* by William J. Locke. John Lane

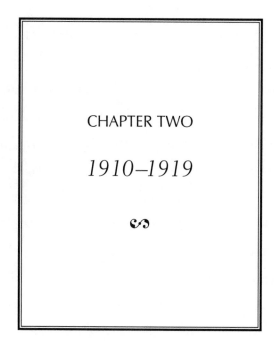

CHAPTER TWO

1910–1919

℘

A LTHOUGH VAST CHANGES were to take place in this decade, the yearly bestseller lists for 1910–1919 do not, at first, reflect them. In Great Britain the death of King Edward VII marked a watershed (and also caused the poet laureate to write some of the worst lines of poetry in the English language: "Over the wire the great news came / He is not much changed, he is very much the same"), but the main shift in American politics did not take place until 1912, with the inauguration of Woodrow Wilson as president.

In 1910, Winston Churchill (the novelist, again, not the English political figure) dropped from his usual place at #1, pushed to #2 by Florence Barclay's *The Rosary,* while Mary Higgins Clark's success was once more prefigured by Mary Roberts Rinehart, who had not one, but *two* mysteries on the year's bestseller list, *The Window at the White Cat* and *When a Man Marries.*

In 1911, *The Rosary* was still on the list, but the main event was Gene Stratton Porter's appearance on the bestseller list, with *The Harvester,* soon to be followed by *Laddie,* marking the start of a long and hugely successful career as a bestseller.

1912 was a watershed of a different kind. Gene Stratton Porter's *The Harvester* continued on the list (as #1), but the big change was that the bestseller list now listed for the first time, separately, nonfiction books as well as novels. From this, we are able to tell rather more about Americans before the First World War than we can merely from reading what novels they bought in quantity. 1912, for example, brought *The Montessori Method,* by Maria Montessori, one of the most influential books on teaching children, and the first of many, many bestsellers over the decades on how to raise a brighter child (hardly anything has been more remunerative to book publishers than the touching and deeply seated American belief that one's children are

brighter than they seem and could be taught better than they are at school),
as well as Albert Paine's biography of Mark Twain (an early "celebrity" biography) and, perhaps most significantly, *How to Live on Twenty-Four Hours a
Day,* by the English writer Arnold Bennett. Here is the first official appearance on the bestseller list of a "self-help" book, which sounds as if it could
have been published successfully at any time in the twenties or thirties, or
even today, and which, as the author of *Power! How to Get It, How to Use It,*
naturally intrigues me. *Woman and Labor,* by Olive Schreiner, and *Creative
Evolution,* by the great French philosopher Henri Bergson, also attest to the
fact that Americans were doing more than reading the novels of Winston
Churchill and Gene Stratton Porter, though both would appear on the 1913
fiction bestseller list, Churchill at #1 again, and Gene Stratton Porter at #3.

1913 also brought the first sign of an awakening interest in European
affairs (not a moment too soon), in the form of the #2 nonfiction bestseller,
Germany and the Germans, by Price Collier, the forerunner, no doubt, of
many similar bestsellers by John Gunther later on, as well as the first book
on contract bridge to hit the list, starting yet another long run that culmi-
nated in the bridge books of Charles Goren. The list, in fact, does not seem
very different from today's—lots of romantic and historical novels; a fiction
bestseller that went on to become a children's classic and to begin a whole
series, *Pollyanna,* by Eleanor H. Porter; a book on policy by the new president, Woodrow Wilson; a business book, *Psychology and Industrial Efficiency,*
by Hugo Munsterberg; and the usual crop of current affairs books.

Of course modern readers would probably find *The Woman Thou
Gavest Me,* by Hall Caine, pretty tame, and *Three Plays,* by Eugène Brieux,
tamer still, though one of them, *Damaged Goods,* was something of a *succès
de scandale* on Broadway, but otherwise it's pretty well the list as we know it.

In 1914, while Europe went to war, *Pollyanna* stayed on the bestseller list for a second year, as did Winston Churchill, while Booth Tarkington's *Penrod* made its appearance on the list at #7, perhaps the only book on the list that anybody is likely to remember today. 1915 brought another novel by Booth Tarkington—apparently almost as quick and prolific a writer as Winston Churchill—a sequel to *Pollyanna,* called (what else?) *Pollyanna Grows Up,* as well as yet another mystery by Mary Roberts Rinehart, and the first appearance on the list of Zane Grey *(The Lone Star Ranger).*

The 1916 list, year of the Battle of the Somme, was topped by Booth Tarkington with *Seventeen,* but was also marked by the first appearance of Kathleen Norris, soon to become a romantic bestseller over and over again, and by H. G. Wells's subtly patriotic family drama *Mr. Britling Sees It Through* (at #4), which did much to show the British side of the war sympathetically to Americans, as several British novelists would do again at the beginning of World War Two. These books were propaganda before the term had taken on its current political meaning, and very astute propaganda, too.

1917 brought America into the war at last and *Mr. Britling Sees It Through* to #1, not coincidentally. The list was now divided into "fiction," "general non-fiction," and a new third category: "war books." General nonfiction included the poems of Alan Seeger ("I Have a Rendezvous with Death" is probably the only one anybody remembers now); *Better Meals for Less Money,* a subject of obvious importance and interest in wartime; *The Plattsburg Manual,* a training manual for would-be officers; and Sir Oliver Lodge's *Raymond,* a book forgotten now, but which, as Alice Payne Hackett points out, by describing his successful attempts to communicate with his dead son, had a certain poignant and obvious appeal at a moment when young men were dying by the hundreds of thousands in the trenches of Picardy and Flanders.

The war books have been pretty much forgotten, together with their authors—the great fiction to come out of World War One would be written by those who survived it, stored up what they had seen and experienced, and lived to write truthfully about it later, as opposed to those who wrote about it while it was going on.

1918 brought a new book by Zane Grey to #1 (*The U.P. Trail*), as well as new novels by the apparently indefatigable Gene Stratton Porter (*A Daughter of the Land*) and Mary Roberts Rinehart. It also marked the first appearance on the list of E. Phillips Oppenheim (with *The Pawns Count*), the first of what was to become one of the major staples of bestselling fiction, the urbane novel of international intrigue, espionage, and adventure, a straight line, as it were, to Tom Clancy, John le Carré, and Clive Cussler.

It is worth noting that with Zane Grey and E. Phillips Oppenheim, there at last appears a category of novels written, by and large, for men. Compare the 1918 fiction list with that of 1913 and you will see a major difference in that respect, doubtless because of the fact that most of army life consists of waiting, and reading novels was one way of passing the time. Thus the sudden appearance of novels written with men in mind as readers that would soon create a whole new category of bestselling fiction.

Alan Seeger continued on the general nonfiction list, as well as *Treasury of War Poetry* and *Rhymes of a Red Cross Man*, all of which argue for a greater interest in poetry than was the case during World War Two, and a book by Douglas Fairbanks may well represent the first movie star bestseller, to be followed by many more. The list of bestselling war books consists once again of books that are mostly forgotten, like *The Glory of the Trenches, Outwitting the Hun, Face to Face With Kaiserism*—these are all fairly obvious works of propaganda—and the 1914–1918 equivalent of Bob Hope's books about entertaining the troops in World War Two, the Korean War, and Vietnam, *A Minstrel in France,* by Harry Lauder, the famous music hall veteran.

1919 was the first year of peace. It brought Gene Stratton Porter, Mary Roberts Rinehart, and Zane Grey back to the list again (already people were getting used to novelists who wrote at least one bestseller a year, and waited eagerly for the next one), but added, more interestingly, Joseph Conrad, a writer of genuine and long-lasting importance, and at #1, one of the most famous of all internationally bestselling novels, *The Four Horsemen of the Apocalypse,* by V. Blasco Ibañez, a book that was made into a hugely successful motion picture starring Rudolph Valentino, and sold in enormous quantities, equivalent, say, to Mario Puzo's *The Godfather* in more recent times. It was also a good read, and a romantic, adventurous novel about the war—the first of its kind—at a moment when the war had not yet become a subject for "popular" fiction, all of which helps to explain its success.

The nonfiction list for 1919 contains at least one major work of enduring importance, at #1, *The Education of Henry Adams,* by Henry Adams, as well as Rudyard Kipling's *The Years Between,* enough to demonstrate that Americans would read "serious" books in large numbers, and also, two years after the abdication of Tsar Nicholas II and one year after the Bolshevik seizure of power in Russia, *Bolshevism,* by John Spargo, the first of many bestselling titles that would explain current events and foreign political movements to American readers.

What is apparent to anybody looking at the bestseller lists for the years 1910 through 1919, is the way in which the books on the bestseller list represent huge and sudden societal changes, the transformation of an innocent and predominantly rural country, which looked inward and backward for literary sustenance, into a country dominated by big cities and by ever more rapid systems of communication, and therefore relatively more open to new trends and ideas.

Though America's involvement in the war was brief—less than two years—the experience precipitated an overwhelming change in American culture and society. Millions of men were drafted, and many of them were sent overseas to France, thus exposing them to new temptations, ideas, and cultural influences. The hit song "How Ya Going to Keep 'Em Down on the Farm? (After They've Seen Paree)" may have been written in a comedic vein, but contained an element of truth, and also asked a question to which there was no easy answer. The complacent small-town world of pre–World War One America (and the books that came out of it, or were written for it) was not yet dead by a long shot—Larry McMurtry was still able to write about it with a mixture of scorn and nostalgia in the 1960s in novels like *The Last Picture Show*—but it had been dealt a deathblow, and at least two generations of American novelists would take it as their task to deride, expose, ridicule, and destroy the kind of ethos small-town America represented. Zane Grey would still be #1 on the list in 1920, but in 1921 Sinclair Lewis's *Main Street* (also a #1 bestseller) ushered in a new and more shocking view of what life in small-town America was like, and revealed the unexpected hunger of American readers for works that had more bite and substance to them than, say, the novels of Gene Stratton Porter.

The fight would not be over in a hurry—it would take the Crash, the Depression, the New Deal, and another world war to complete the route— but the lines were already drawn between those demanding new freedoms (to write, as well as everything else), and those trying to preserve an America whose roots were still planted firmly in the nineteenth century. Of course there would still be plenty of readers for "romantic" fiction of the old-fashioned kind—there still are—and the appearance of Temple Bailey on the

1919 list at #8 is a sign of that, but even as she made her way onto the list (with *The Tin Soldier*), Hemingway, Fitzgerald, and Pound were already beginning to write, and casting an unforgiving, if sometimes envious, eye on the world of their fathers—and of their mothers and sisters.

For women, too, had, in a sense, been "liberated," however inadvertently, by war work, by learning to live without their husbands, by the kind of heightened sexuality that accompanies war, and by the vast and bewildering changes that engulfed America as the automobile brought with it paved roads, the freedom of getting in the car and going somewhere, anywhere, the first suburbs, sex in the backseat. It was not just the automobile—the movies brought glamour to people who had never been exposed to it; popular magazines with photographs made them aware of fashions more exotic than those that could be found on Main Street and in the Sears, Roebuck catalog; the radio brought them entertainment at home, and instant news; the phonograph brought them the latest music and dance tunes; everywhere one looked science and technology were breaking down the insulating walls that had protected small-town Americans from big-city temptations, fads, and habits. The dislocations of war would soon bring about even greater changes—women's determination to have smaller families would lead to a critical struggle over birth control and books that advocated birth control, while the exposure of countless Americans to "Paree," or at any rate to European culture, would bring about not only a new frankness about sex in fiction, but in the end, a whole new school of writing, a literature that would eventually rival anything the Europeans themselves produced in the 1930s and 1940s, and that turned away deliberately from the sentimentality, complacency, and primness that had hitherto characterized American fiction. Young writers were rejecting the kind of world about which Gene Stratton

Porter had been writing just as decisively as American women had rejected the world of their mothers by flinging away their corsets, adopting short skirts and rolled stockings, cropping their hair, using lipstick, and smoking cigarettes in public. They wanted freedom, and not surprisingly they wanted books that mirrored their own hungers and desires and interest in the world.

It would take them a while to get them. The world of books was rooted in old traditions, and moved more slowly than that of the movies, and book publishers and bookstores were nervous about anything new or daring, in fiction and in nonfiction alike, and vulnerable not only to their own prejudices and opinions, but to formidable pressures from official and self-appointed censors. The phrase "banned in Boston" would soon be the code for a racy work of fiction, or a nonfiction book about sex education or birth control, but despite formal and informal censorship, change was in the air. The country was enjoying a wild burst of prosperity (albeit pretty much limited to the urban white middle class, the upper-middle class, and the rich), and the world of book publishing would very shortly be rocked by the advent of new publishing houses, many of them founded by Jews who were not welcome in the old-fashioned, traditionally WASP world of publishing—Boni & Liveright was the first of these new publishers, followed by Alfred A. Knopf, Random House, Simon & Schuster, and Viking. The new publishers were willing to take bigger risks—they had to be—they were determined to advertise and promote books in new ways, and they were helped in their task by the creation of the first national news magazine, Henry Luce's *Time,* which treated books as news, and by the *Reader's Digest,* which excerpted them, as well as by alliances with the radio networks and the motion picture corporations, and by the invention of the book club, which brought the book, at steep discounts, to millions of people who lived far from the nearest bookshop.

1910

FICTION

1. *The Rosary,* by Florence Barclay. Putnam

2. *A Modern Chronicle,* by Winston Churchill. Macmillan

3. *The Wild Olive,* Anonymous (Basil King). Harper

4. *Max,* by Katherine Cecil Thurston. Harper

5. *The Kingdom of Slender Swords,* by Hallie Erminíe Rives. Bobbs-Merrill

6. *Simon the Jester,* by William J. Locke. John Lane

7. *Lord Loveland Discovers America,* by C. N. and A. M. Williamson. Doubleday, Page

8. *The Window at the White Cat,* by Mary Roberts Rinehart. Bobbs-Merrill

9. *Molly Make-Believe,* by Eleanor Abbott. Century

10. *When a Man Marries,* by Mary Roberts Rinehart. Bobbs-Merrill

1911

FICTION

1. *The Broad Highway,* by Jeffrey Farnol. Little, Brown

2. *The Prodigal Judge,* by Vaughan Kester. Bobbs-Merrill

3. *The Winning of Barbara Worth,* by Harold Bell Wright. Book Supply Co.

4. *Queed,* by Henry Sydnor Harrison. Houghton Mifflin

5. *The Harvester,* by Gene Stratton Porter. Doubleday, Page

6. *The Iron Woman,* by Margaret Deland. Harper

7. *The Long Roll,* by Mary Johnston. Houghton Mifflin

8. *Molly Make-Believe,* by Eleanor Abbott. Century

9. *The Rosary,* by Florence Barclay. Putnam

10. *The Common Law,* by Robert W. Chambers. Appleton

1912

FICTION

1. *The Harvester,* by Gene Stratton Porter. Doubleday, Page

2. *The Street Called Straight,* by Basil King. Harper

3. *Their Yesterdays,* by Harold Bell Wright. Book Supply Co.

4. *The Melting of Molly,* by Maria Thompson Daviess. Bobbs-Merrill

5. *A Hoosier Chronicle,* by Meredith Nicholson. Houghton Mifflin

6. *The Winning of Barbara Worth,* by Harold Bell Wright. Book Supply Co.

7. *The Just and the Unjust,* by Vaughan Kester. Bobbs-Merrill

8. *The Net,* by Rex Beach. Harper

9. *Tante,* by Anne Douglas Sedgwick. Century

10. *Fran,* by J. Breckenridge Ellis. Bobbs-Merrill

NONFICTION

1. *The Promised Land,* by Mary Antin. Houghton Mifflin

2. *The Montessori Method,* by Maria Montessori. Stokes

3. *South America,* by James Bryce. Macmillan

4. *A New Conscience and an Ancient Evil,* by Jane Addams. Macmillan

5. *Three Plays,* by Eugène Brieux. Brentano

6. *Your United States,* by Arnold Bennett. Harper

7. *Creative Evolution,* by Henri Bergson. Holt

8. *How to Live on Twenty-Four Hours a Day,* by Arnold Bennett. Doran

9. *Woman and Labor,* by Olive Schreiner. Stokes

10. *Mark Twain,* by Albert Bigelow Paine. Harper

1913

FICTION

1. *The Inside of the Cup,* by Winston Churchill. Macmillan

2. *V.V.'s Eyes,* by Henry Sydnor Harrison. Houghton Mifflin

3. *Laddie,* by Gene Stratton Porter. Doubleday, Page

4. *The Judgment House,* by Sir Gilbert Parker. Harper

5. *Heart of the Hills,* by John Fox Jr. Scribner

6. *The Amateur Gentleman,* by Jeffrey Farnol. Little, Brown

7. *The Woman Thou Gavest Me,* by Hall Caine. Lippincott

8. *Pollyanna,* by Eleanor H. Porter. Page

9. *The Valiants of Virginia,* by Hallie Erminíe Rives. Bobbs-Merrill

10. *T. Tembarom,* by Frances Hodgson Burnett. Century

NONFICTION

1. *Crowds,* by Gerald Stanley Lee. Doubleday, Page

2. *Germany and the Germans,* by Price Collier. Scribner

3. *Zone Policeman 88,* by Harry A. Franck. Century

4. *The New Freedom,* by Woodrow Wilson. Doubleday, Page

5. *South America,* by James Bryce. Macmillan

6. *Your United States,* by Arnold Bennett. Harper

7. *The Promised Land,* by Mary Antin. Houghton Mifflin

8. *Auction Bridge To-Day,* by Milton C. Work. Houghton Mifflin

9. *Three Plays,* by Eugène Brieux. Brentano

10. *Psychology and Industrial Efficiency,* by Hugo Munsterberg. Houghton Mifflin

1914

FICTION

1. *The Eyes of the World,* by Harold Bell Wright. Book Supply Co.

2. *Pollyanna,* by Eleanor H. Porter. Page

3. *The Inside of the Cup,* by Winston Churchill. Macmillan

4. *The Salamander,* by Owen Johnson. Bobbs-Merrill

5. *The Fortunate Youth,* by William J. Locke. John Lane

6. *T. Tembarom,* by Frances Hodgson Burnett. Century

7. *Penrod,* by Booth Tarkington. Doubleday, Page

8. *Diane of the Green Van,* by Leona Dalrymple. Reilly & Britton

9. *The Devil's Garden,* by W. B. Maxwell. Bobbs-Merrill

10. *The Prince of Graustark,* by George Barr McCutcheon. Dodd, Mead

1915

FICTION

1. *The Turmoil,* by Booth Tarkington. Harper

2. *A Far Country,* by Winston Churchill. Macmillan

3. *Michael O'Halloran,* by Gene Stratton Porter. Doubleday, Page

4. *Pollyanna Grows Up,* by Eleanor H. Porter. Page

5. *K,* by Mary Roberts Rinehart. Houghton Mifflin

6. *Jaffery,* by William J. Locke. John Lane

7. *Felix O'Day,* by F. Hopkinson Smith. Scribner

8. *The Harbor,* by Ernest Poole. Macmillan

9. *The Lone Star Ranger,* by Zane Grey. Harper

10. *Angela's Business,* by Henry Sydnor Harrison. Houghton Mifflin

1916

FICTION

1. *Seventeen,* by Booth Tarkington. Harper

2. *When a Man's a Man,* by Harold Bell Wright. Book Supply Co.

3. *Just David,* by Eleanor H. Porter. Houghton Mifflin

4. *Mr. Britling Sees It Through,* by H. G. Wells. Macmillan

5. *Life and Gabriella,* by Ellen Glasgow. Doubleday, Page

6. *The Real Adventure,* by Henry Kitchell Webster. Bobbs-Merrill

7. *Bars of Iron,* by Ethel M. Dell. Putnam

8. *Nan of Music Mountain,* by Frank H. Spearman. Scribner

9. *Dear Enemy,* by Jean Webster. Century

10. *The Heart of Rachael,* by Kathleen Norris. Doubleday, Page

1917

FICTION

1. *Mr. Britling Sees It Through,* by H. G. Wells. Macmillan

2. *The Light in the Clearing,* by Irving Bacheller. Bobbs-Merrill

3. *The Red Planet,* by William J. Locke. John Lane

4. *The Road to Understanding,* by Eleanor H. Porter. Houghton Mifflin

5. *Wildfire,* by Zane Grey. Harper

6. *Christine,* by Alice Cholmondeley. Macmillan

7. *In the Wilderness,* by Robert S. Hichens. Stokes

8. *His Family,* by Ernest Poole. Macmillan

9. *The Definite Object,* by Jeffery Farnol. Little, Brown

10. *The Hundredth Chance,* by Ethel M. Dell. Putnam

GENERAL NONFICTION

1. *Rhymes of a Red Cross Man,* by Robert W. Service. Barse & Hopkins

2. *The Plattsburg Manual,* by O. O. Ellis and E. B. Garey. Century

3. *Raymond,* by Sir Oliver Lodge. Doran

4. *Poems of Alan Seeger.* Scribner

5. *God the Invisible King,* by H. G. Wells. Macmillan

6. *Laugh and Live,* by Douglas Fairbanks. Britton Publishing Co.

7. *Better Meals for Less Money,* by Mary Green. Holt

WAR BOOKS

1. *The First Hundred Thousand,* by Ian Hay. Houghton Mifflin

2. *My Home in the Field of Honor,* by Frances W. Huard. Doran

3. *A Student in Arms,* by Donald Hankey. Dutton

4. *Over the Top,* by Arthur Guy Empey. Putnam

5. *Carry On,* by Coningsby Dawson. John Lane

6. *Getting Together,* by Ian Hay. Houghton Mifflin

7. *My Second Year of the War,* by Frederick Palmer. Dodd, Mead

8. *The Land of Deepening Shadow,* by D. Thomas Curtin. Doran

9. *Italy, France and Britain at War,* by H. G. Wells. Macmillan

10. *The Worn Doorstep,* by Margaret Sherwood. Little, Brown

1918

FICTION

1. *The U. P. Trail,* by Zane Grey. Harper

2. *The Tree of Heaven,* by May Sinclair. Macmillan

3. *The Amazing Interlude,* by Mary Roberts Rinehart. Doran

4. *Dere Mable,* by Edward Streeter. Stokes

5. *Oh, Money! Money!* by Eleanor H. Porter. Houghton Mifflin

6. *Greatheart,* by Ethel M. Dell. Putnam

7. *The Major,* by Ralph Connor. Revell

8. *The Pawns Count,* by E. Phillips Oppenheim. Little, Brown

9. *A Daughter of the Land,* by Gene Stratton Porter. Doubleday, Page

10. *Sonia,* by Stephen McKenna. Doran

GENERAL NONFICTION

1. *Rhymes of a Red Cross Man,* by Robert W. Service. Barse & Hopkins

2. *Treasury of War Poetry,* by G. H. Clark. Houghton Mifflin

3. *With the Colors,* by Everard J. Appleton. Stewart, Kidd

4. *Recollections,* by Viscount Morley. Macmillan

5. *Laugh and Live,* by Douglas Fairbanks. Britton Publishing Co.

6. *Mark Twain's Letters,* ed. by Albert Bigelow Paine. Harper

7. *Adventures and Letters of Richard Harding Davis,* by Richard Harding Davis. Scribner

8. *Over Here,* by Edgar Guest. Reilly & Lee

9. *Diplomatic Days,* by Edith O'Shaughnessy. Harper

10. *Poems of Alan Seeger.* Scribner

WAR BOOKS

1. *My Four Years in Germany,* by James W. Gerard. Doran

2. *The Glory of the Trenches,* by Coningsby Dawson. John Lane

3. *Over the Top,* by Arthur Guy Empey. Putnam

4. *A Minstrel in France,* by Harry Lauder. Hearst's International Library Co.

5. *Private Peat,* by Harold R. Peat. Bobbs-Merrill

6. *Outwitting the Hun,* by Lieut. Pat O'Brien. Harper

7. *Face to Face With Kaiserism,* by James W. Gerard. Doran

8. *Carry On,* by Coningsby Dawson. John Lane

9. *Out to Win,* by Coningsby Dawson. John Lane

10. *Under Fire,* by Henri Barbusse. Dutton

1919

FICTION

1. *The Four Horsemen of the Apocalypse,* by V. Blasco Ibañez. Dutton

2. *The Arrow of Gold,* by Joseph Conrad. Doubleday, Page

3. *The Desert of Wheat,* by Zane Grey. Harper

4. *Dangerous Days,* by Mary Roberts Rinehart. Doran

5. *The Sky Pilot in No Man's Land,* by Ralph Connor. Doran

6. *The Re-Creation of Brian Kent,* by Harold Bell Wright. Book Supply Co.

7. *Dawn,* by Gene Stratton Porter. Houghton Mifflin

8. *The Tin Soldier,* by Temple Bailey. Penn Publishing Co.

9. *Christopher and Columbus,* by "Elizabeth." Doubleday, Page

10. *In Secret,* by Robert W. Chambers. Doran

NONFICTION

1. *The Education of Henry Adams,* by Henry Adams. Houghton Mifflin

2. *The Years Between,* by Rudyard Kipling. Doubleday, Page

3. *Belgium,* by Brand Whitlock. Appleton

4. *The Seven Purposes,* by Margaret Cameron. Harper

5. *In Flanders Fields,* by John McCrae. Putnam

6. *Bolshevism,* by John Spargo. Harper

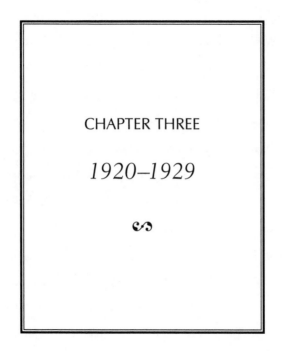

CHAPTER THREE

1920–1929

ख

THE BESTSELLER LIST for the first year of the new decade showed a certain clinging to the past. E. Phillips Oppenheim was back on the list (at #8), Zane Grey was once again at #1 (showing that men were now in the habit of buying novels), while Ethel M. Dell, a newcomer to the list, showed that romance was still in vogue among women readers, as well as the appearance of yet another Kathleen Norris novel.

In nonfiction, however, *The Economic Consequences of the Peace,* by John Maynard Keynes, perhaps one of the most important and prescient of post–World War One books, reached #2, though subsequently the Crash, world depression, and the rise of Nazism would seem to indicate that while a lot of people *read* Keynes, not many of them took his warnings seriously, or possibly they simply failed to understand them. Two books about Theodore Roosevelt showed America's nostalgia for the man, even though they had failed to vote for him in 1912, while Frederick O'Brien's *White Shadows in the South Seas* prefigured whole archipelagos of books on exploring the South Pacific, perhaps the most memorable of which would be *Kon-Tiki,* in 1950. 1921 brought Sinclair Lewis's *Main Street* to #1, as well as Edith Wharton's *The Age of Innocence,* a book that has survived the test of time better than most. Gene Stratton Porter was still on the list, as well as Mary Roberts Rinehart, but so far as fiction is concerned, the year was memorable for the publication of perhaps the most romantic trashy bestselling novel of all time, *The Sheik,* by Edith M. Hull, which would be made into a movie starring Rudolph Valentino. The book seems to have launched the primary woman's erotic fantasy of the early twenties, and ushered in, though it may not have seemed so at the time, a genre of fiction publishing that was a good deal more racy than previous "romantic" fiction (though still pretty tame by the standards of our day). 1922 saw *The Sheik* on the list for the second year, along with what were now the usual yearly new bestsellers from Zane Grey and Mary Roberts Rinehart, and, more significantly, a new novel from Sinclair Lewis, *Babbitt*.

The nonfiction bestseller list shows an America confronting "modern" problems and ideas. H. G. Wells's *The Outline of History* was #1, just ahead of Hendrik Willem Van Loon's *The Story of Mankind*, both the kind of big, optimistic works of history that were to prove popular over the next few decades, as well as Lytton Strachey's *Queen Victoria*, a by no means flattering royal portrait, and the first of many to portray the royal family as something less than perfect. *Diet and Health* and *Outwitting Our Nerves* demonstrate that, then as now, Americans were prepared to put down their money for any book that promised weight loss or serenity.

1923 brought the usual mix in fiction, with a new Mary Roberts Rinehart book, a new Zane Grey, and a #1 bestseller from the veteran Gertrude Atherton, but it was again in nonfiction that one can sense the change in the interests of the average American reader. The climb from immigrant status and manners, and from working class to middle class, triggered by the increase in prosperity and "white-collar" employment, brought to the top of the list one of the great bestsellers of all time, Emily Post's *Etiquette*, as well as *Diet and Health*, by Lulu Hunt Peters, and *Self-Mastery Through Conscious Auto-Suggestion*, by Emile Coué, the first of those successful "self-help" books that reached their apogee in the 1970s with books like *I'm OK, You're OK*. Coué's system involved repeating over and over again to oneself, "Every day, in every way, I am getting better and better." All over America, people could be heard muttering this to themselves, long before the word "mantra" had entered the language, and Coué, long before the television talk show had been even imagined, became the first of a new phenomenon: the foreign guru for ordinary Americans, with his message contained in a bestselling book.

1924 saw two major phenomena appear on the bestseller list. The first was the appearance at #1 on the fiction list of *So Big,* by Edna Ferber, in some ways the first really recognizable modern fiction bestseller, with a promotable author, a "modern" story, and a big subject. Ferber's books were at once fast-paced stories with bigger-than-life characters, and carefully researched reports on major areas or subjects of American life. Her books, in fact, prepared the way both for James Michener's bestsellers and Irving Wallace's, though it has to be said that Ferber at her best, in, say, *Giant* or *The Ice Palace* or *Cimarron,* was more fun than either of them, or even than both of them put together.

The second was the infant Simon & Schuster's first book, *The Cross Word Puzzle Book,* which took America by storm, and started a whole new craze for what would later be called "nonbooks," i.e., books that aren't made to be read. Bookstores were at first unwilling to stock the first crossword book—all the more so since it came with a pencil attached to it on a string—but once the craze caught on, they sold hundreds of thousands, and since then have learned to live with "merchandise," whether in the form of puzzles, calendars, or "pop-up" books. Even Simon & Schuster displayed a certain initial embarrassment at the nature of their first venture, and it was at first published by "Plaza Publishers," a name taken from their New York telephone exchange, in case the more "serious" authors they hoped to attract would be put off by the puzzle book, but in the event, S&S acquired a reputation for canny marketing and publicity that gave them an edge over older, more staid book publishers for many years, and the "Plaza" name was quietly dropped.

The 1924 list also reveals another big change in American life—the almost exponential growth of American interest in science, typified by the presence on the list of *The New Decalogue of Science,* by Albert E. Wiggam, by no means an easy book to crack (and not exactly a catchy title, either).

The presence of the distinguished playwright and iconoclast George Bernard Shaw and of the French biographer André Maurois on the list is also evidence of an increasing sophistication, and a growing openness to new ideas and to foreign writers. Faster (and ever more luxurious) ocean liners were bringing Americans to England and Europe in ever larger numbers, and a trip to Europe was no longer the prerogative of the wealthy and the privileged few. At the same time, writers and celebrities like Shaw had discovered the value of American publicity, and the ease of getting it (if you had any kind of fame or news value at home, all you had to do was cross the Atlantic in five or six days on a steamer, and arrive in New York to be interviewed and photographed by the whole New York City press corps).

Long before American authors had realized the value of personal publicity, the British had learned how to use it to sell books here, starting, after all, with Dickens and going on to Oscar Wilde. The recipe was simple, if exhausting: You gave lectures all over America; were interviewed by the major papers; got yourself photographed, as Shaw did and as Winston Churchill (the politician and historian, this time) would shortly do, visiting a Hollywood studio, or having dinner at San Simeon with William Randolph Hearst, or being greeted by an Indian chief; and before you could say, "Hey presto!" your book was selling in huge numbers and you went home to collect huge royalties, plus fat profits from the lecture circuit. Lectures paid good money, sold books, and led to reams of personal publicity, and in every town where you lectured there was bound to be a bookstore with a display of your book(s), ready to be signed. The puzzle is that foreigners were the only ones who twigged to this magic combination at first, but it shortly became the very heart and soul of the book business, prompting publishers and booksellers to ask whether an author was promotable rather than whether he or she could write.

Of course the ideal was somebody like Shaw or Churchill, who was promotable *and* could write, but in the meantime the outlines of book publishing in the future were there for all to see. First the book had become merchandise; then the author had become the means of selling his or her book, with the big bucks going to the authors who were already famous or who could sum up what their book was about in one pithy phrase, and who could stand in a receiving line for hours smiling and exchanging greetings with total strangers. It is not surprising that theater people like Shaw, or professional politicians like Churchill, were good at it—this was their stock in trade, after all. In future, the successful author would need a politician's ability to make speeches and press the flesh, and an actor's ability to project enthusiasm, energy, and interest, at least in his or her own work and ideas. The days when it was the author's job to sit at a desk and write, and leave the selling of the book to the publisher and the bookstores, were coming to an end, long before radio and television played a role. The bookstore came of age as the place where the whole process of publishing and author promotion came down to its final purpose, as money changed hands. Or, in some cases, failed to.

The emergence of the bookstore as a serious place of commerce was very much a part of the period. Prior to then, selling books had been, to put it very mildly, one of the quieter areas of commerce, and not much was required in the way of salesmanship or marketing—certainly nothing in the way of showmanship. The advent of the celebrity author soon changed all that. The dim, hushed, library-like atmosphere of the traditional bookstore, with its dark paneling and poor lighting, gave way to the first modern bookstores, with big plate glass windows and plenty of display space—a contrast that can be appreciated today in midtown New York City by comparing the Rizzoli Book Store on 57th Street with the big Barnes & Noble "flagship" store on Fifth Avenue. The Rizzoli store is designed to resemble a pre-1920s bookstore, dark wood, elegant, hushed, while the B&N store is brightly lit, with a high-tech checkout area. It was in the 1920s that bookstores began to put on the display tables not just "new books," but specifically "best sellers," sometimes with a copy of the list, and to sell merchandise at the cash register. The tendency to present books by displaying them on tables, instead of simply lining them up on shelves, very often with only the spine showing, soon led publishers to pay more attention to the book jacket as a marketing tool, instead of its being referred to, and thought of, as "the dust jacket," something the publisher had hitherto put on the book to keep it clean and that most people took off the moment they got the book home. Except in the most old-fashioned of book publishers, jacket design became a serious matter, and the profession of "art director" found its way into publishing, as well as the habit, when it came to bestsellers and art books, of asking key booksellers what they thought of a jacket design.

1925 brought to the stores Michael Arlen's daring and fashionable novel *The Green Hat,* a book that perfectly suited the zeitgeist of the twenties (and now seems strangely old-fashioned), like the early plays of Noël Coward, but that sold well enough to bring it to #5, in a year that included Sinclair Lewis's *Arrowsmith,* yet another novel by Gene Stratton Porter, and a quiver full of historical novels and romances. *The Cross Word Puzzle Book* was still on the nonfiction list, as Simon & Schuster sheepishly tried to develop a reputation for something else, but a diet book was #1, while the #2 spot went to a cookbook, edited by Fannie Farmer, who rapidly became America's favorite (and most famous) cook. Perhaps the most famous nonfiction book of the twenties was published in 1925, advertising executive Bruce Barton's *The Man Nobody Knows,* which celebrated Christ as a muscular and dynamic CEO and salesman who picked twelve men as his top executives and went on to found one of the world's largest, most enduring, and most successful organizations. The notion of portraying Christ as a successful business executive—and, by reversing the analogy, portraying the modern American business executive as performing a Christian act by doing business—was one that was already starting to make people giggle three years later, when America's top business executives had plunged the country into the Great Depression and were no longer seen as Christ-like, but it was typical of the two sides of the twenties: on the one hand, a profound need for the new and startling, so that even religion had to be presented in a different way to succeed, and on the other, an amazing confidence that money and success were God-given and good for the soul, that it was now easy (and right) for a rich man to pass through the eye of a needle and enter the kingdom of heaven, and that prosperity was not just its own reward, but virtuous as well. This illusion ended sharply in 1929, but you can trace the outlines of it in the bestseller lists of the late twenties easily enough.

1926 brought to #1 on the best seller list *The Private Life of Helen of Troy,* by John Erskine, a book that was the forerunner of a new kind of historical fiction, less romantic than debunking, and which my uncle Alexander Korda was to make into a movie starring my aunt Maria Corda in Hollywood in 1928, an event that brought happiness to nobody, since Alex hated Hollywood and also separated from the tempestuous Maria. The idea of the movie caught on, however, and Alex would eventually make the hugely successful *The Private Life of Henry VIII* (starring Charles Laughton) and the somewhat less successful *The Private Life of Don Juan* (starring Douglas Fairbanks). At #2 was another bestselling book that leapt to even greater fame as a movie, *Gentlemen Prefer Blondes,* by Anita Loos, and three more bestsellers that would be filmed as great successes, *Beau Geste, Beau Sabreur,* and the immortal *Show Boat,* by Edna Ferber.

The bestseller list was already starting to be the mine from which movie stories were hewn, though sound was still two years away. *Gentlemen Prefer Blondes* went on to succeed in several incarnations, on stage and in the movies, the last one starring Marilyn Monroe, while *Show Boat* went on to become something of a national institution. The bestseller list became overnight an object of close study on the part of film studios and movie producers, and a whole new profession sprang up overnight of East Coast story editors, whose job was to monitor the list for stories and, in general, take publishers and editors out to lunch in search of a first look at a "hot book," as well as agents who actually *read* books (or at least hired somebody to read them), the first and most successful of the long line being Leland Hayward, father of Brooke Hayward, who became a bestselling author herself, followed by Myron Selznick, David O. Selznick's brother, and Irving Paul ("Swifty") Lazar, all of whom aspired to be the one who would bring to the studios the early draft of a hot novel before anybody in Hollywood had read it. The list was now followed, on both coasts, with the kind of attention that people were paying to the daily list of stock prices, but with less unhappy results in the end.

1927 brought Sinclair Lewis's *Elmer Gantry* to #1, as well as confirming the fact that Mary Roberts Rinehart was still going strong. In nonfiction, it was a bumper crop—Simon & Schuster recovered from its embarrassment over its debut with crosswords by making Will Durant's *The Story of Philosophy* a #1 bestseller, on a list that included such relatively heavyweight contenders as *We,* by Charles Lindbergh, *Revolt in the Desert,* by T. E. Lawrence, and *Napoleon,* by Emil Ludwig. Once again Americans were showing an ability to absorb long, serious, and difficult novels, and to tackle novels like *Elmer Gantry* that were controversial and not by any stretch of the imagination fluffy or romantic reading. In short, a scan of the bestseller list shows us an America of serious readers, coinciding with that of people who read romantic novels or read the travel escapism of Richard Halliburton, who had two books on the list.

1928 brought to the top of the bestseller list Thornton Wilder's *The Bridge of San Luis Rey,* another novel that has survived the test of time. On the nonfiction list, George Bernard Shaw's *The Intelligent Woman's Guide to Socialism and Capitalism* hit the list, only a year before the collapse of the stock market left a lot of people of both sexes wondering whether capitalism made sense.

1929 brought with it the starling revelation, which has cheered publishers and bookstores ever since, that people would go on buying books even in a depression. Erich Maria Remarque's *All Quiet on the Western Front* was the #1 fiction bestseller, and was taken by most people as a sign that there would never be another great war (just ten years before World War Two broke out), while on the nonfiction list the fledgling Simon & Schuster's gift for catchy nonfiction was signaled by the presence on the list of four bestsellers, Ernest Dimnet's *The Art of Thinking* (#1), Joan Lowell's *The Cradle of the Deep,* Robert L. Ripley's *Believe It or Not,* and Will Durant's *The Mansions of Philosophy.* Few things better illustrate the tastes and interests of Americans than these books—Dimnet's book was dense and difficult, Joan Lowell's was a sailing adventure of doubtful veracity, Ripley's *Believe It or Not* became a national sensation and went on for decades, a solid piece of merchandise at every bookstore, and Durant proved once again that Americans would read serious history and even philosophy if it were offered to them with the right kind of enthusiasm. The founding of the book clubs made the sales of some of these books, Durant's particularly, much larger than the bookstore sale alone, and bookstores, which were at first opposed to the whole idea, soon came to embrace it—book clubs created more readers, more readers eventually became more customers, and a major book club selection by the Literary Guild or the august judges of the Book-of-the-Month Club became a major selling point for books, analogous to *Good Housekeeping*'s Seal of Approval for houseware products.

Perhaps the most extraordinary and longest-lasting book on the list was *The Specialist,* by Chic Sale, a self-published little book about a guy whose specialty was building outhouses, which went on to sell over 1,500,000 copies, and for years sat beside the cash register at every bookstore in America. Perhaps its success denoted some nostalgia for a simpler rural past, or for the certainties of an older, simpler America, before the twenties took everybody on a dizzying roller-coaster ride, then brought them crashing down again.

In any event, people continued to read, even as their stock portfolios lay in shreds—indeed for many of the investing class, staying at home with a book was about all they could afford to do, after a decade of speakeasies and wild parties. The Crash turned them toward the more serious things, like history, biography, philosophy, in a search perhaps of some proof that the world had once made sense, or made sense to somebody, and of some other, more profound and lasting, meaning to life than the rise (and drastic fall) of stocks. The eternal verities were high on the list now, as people looked for something to sustain them in a world that seemed to be crumbling around them.

Of course, as Jimmy Durante used to say, "You ain't seen nothin' yet!" The thirties would replace the sudden pain of the Crash with long misery, loss of faith in "the system," the rise of Fascism and Nazism, and, once again, the fear of war. There would, in short, be plenty to read about and plenty to seek escape from.

1920

FICTION

1. *The Man of the Forest,* by Zane Grey. Harper

2. *Kindred of the Dust,* by Peter B. Kyne. Cosmopolitan Book Co.

3. *The Re-Creation of Brian Kent,* by Harold Bell Wright. Book Supply Co.

4. *The River's End,* by James Oliver Curwood. Cosmopolitan Book Co.

5. *A Man for the Ages,* by Irving Bacheller. Bobbs-Merrill

6. *Mary-Marie,* by Eleanor H. Porter. Houghton Mifflin

7. *The Portygee,* by Joseph C. Lincoln. Appleton

8. *The Great Impersonation,* by E. Phillips Oppenheim. Little, Brown

9. *The Lamp in the Desert,* by Ethel M. Dell. Putnam

10. *Harriet and the Piper,* by Kathleen Norris. Doubleday, Page

NONFICTION

1. *Now It Can Be Told,* by Philip Gibbs. Harper

2. *The Economic Consequences of the Peace,* by John M. Keynes. Harcourt, Brace

3. *Roosevelt's Letters to His Children,* ed. by Joseph B. Bishop. Scribner

4. *Theodore Roosevelt,* by William Roscoe Thayer. Scribner

5. *White Shadows in the South Seas,* by Frederick O'Brien. Century

6. *An American Idyll,* by Cornelia Stratton Parker. Atlantic Monthly Press

1921

FICTION

1. *Main Street,* by Sinclair Lewis. Harcourt, Brace

2. *The Brimming Cup,* by Dorothy Canfield. Harcourt, Brace

3. *The Mysterious Rider,* by Zane Grey. Harper

4. *The Age of Innocence,* by Edith Wharton. Appleton

5. *The Valley of Silent Men,* by James Oliver Curwood. Cosmopolitan Book Co.

6. *The Sheik,* by Edith M. Hull. Small, Maynard

7. *A Poor Wise Man,* by Mary Roberts Rinehart. Doran

8. *Her Father's Daughter,* by Gene Stratton Porter. Doubleday, Page

9. *The Sisters-in-Law,* by Gertrude Atherton. Stokes

10. *The Kingdom Round the Corner,* by Coningsby Dawson. Cosmopolitan Book Co.

NONFICTION

1. *The Outline of History,* by H. G. Wells. Macmillan

2. *White Shadows in the South Seas,* by Frederick O'Brien. Century

3. *The Mirrors of Downing Street, by a Gentleman with a Duster* (Harold Begbie). Putnam

4. *Mystic Isles of the South Seas,* by Frederick O'Brien. Century

5. *The Autobiography of Margot Asquith.* Doran

6. *Peace Negotiations,* by Robert Lansing. Houghton Mifflin

1922

FICTION

1. *If Winter Comes,* by A. S. M. Hutchinson. Little, Brown

2. *The Sheik,* by Edith M. Hull. Small, Maynard

3. *Gentle Julia,* by Booth Tarkington. Doubleday, Page

4. *The Head of the House of Coombe,* by Frances Hodgson Burnett. Stokes

5. *Simon Called Peter,* by Robert Keable. Dutton

6. *The Breaking Point,* by Mary Roberts Rinehart. Doran

7. *This Freedom*, by A. S. M. Hutchinson. Little, Brown

8. *Maria Chapdelaine,* by Louis Hémon. Macmillan

9. *To the Last Man,* by Zane Grey. Harper

10. *Babbitt,* by Sinclair Lewis. Harcourt, Brace

    Helen of the Old House, by Harold Bell Wright. Appleton

NONFICTION

1. *The Outline of History,* by H. G. Wells. Macmillan

2. *The Story of Mankind,* by Hendrik Willem Van Loon. Boni & Liveright

3. *The Americanization of Edward Bok,* by Edward Bok. Scribner

4. *Diet and Health,* by Lulu Hunt Peters. Reilly & Lee

5. *The Mind in the Making,* by James Harvey Robinson. Harper

6. *The Outline of Science,* by J. Arthur Thomson. Putnam

7. *Outwitting Our Nerves,* by Josephine A. Jackson and Helen M. Salisbury. Century

8. *Queen Victoria,* by Lytton Strachey. Harcourt, Brace

9. *Mirrors of Washington,* Anonymous (Clinton W. Gilbert). Putnam

10. *Painted Windows, by a Gentleman with a Duster* (Harold Begbie). Putnam

1923

FICTION

1. *Black Oxen,* by Gertrude Atherton. Boni & Liveright

2. *His Children's Children,* by Arthur Train. Scribner

3. *The Enchanted April,* by "Elizabeth." Doubleday, Page

4. *Babbitt,* by Sinclair Lewis. Harcourt, Brace

5. *The Dim Lantern,* by Temple Bailey. Penn Publishing Co.

6. *This Freedom,* by A. S. M. Hutchinson. Little, Brown

7. *The Mine with the Iron Door,* by Harold Bell Wright. Appleton

8. *The Wanderer of the Wasteland,* by Zane Grey. Harper

9. *The Sea-Hawk,* by Rafael Sabatini. Houghton Mifflin

10. *The Breaking Point,* by Mary Roberts Rinehart. Doran

NONFICTION

1. *Etiquette,* by Emily Post. Funk & Wagnalls

2. *The Life of Christ,* by Giovanni Papini. Harcourt, Brace

3. *The Life and Letters of Walter H. Page,* ed. by Burton J. Hendrick. Doubleday, Page

4. *The Mind in the Making,* by James Harvey Robinson. Harper

5. *The Outline of History,* by H. G. Wells. Macmillan

6. *Diet and Health,* by Lulu Hunt Peters. Reilly & Lee

7. *Self-Mastery Through Conscious Auto-Suggestion,* by Emile Coué. American Library Service

8. *The Americanization of Edward Bok,* by Edward Bok. Scribner

9. *The Story of Mankind,* by Hendrik Willem Van Loon. Boni & Liveright

10. *A Man from Maine,* by Edward Bok. Scribner

1924

FICTION

1. *So Big,* by Edna Ferber. Doubleday, Page

2. *The Plastic Age,* by Percy Marks. Century

3. *The Little French Girl,* by Anne Douglas Sedgwick. Houghton Mifflin

4. *The Heirs Apparent,* by Philip Gibbs. Doran

5. *A Gentleman of Courage,* by James Oliver Curwood. Cosmopolitan Book Co.

6. *The Call of the Canyon,* by Zane Grey. Harper

7. *The Midlander,* by Booth Tarkington. Doubleday, Page

8. *The Coast of Folly,* by Coningsby Dawson. Cosmopolitan Book Co.

9. *Mistress Wilding,* by Rafael Sabatini. Houghton Mifflin

10. *The Homemaker,* by Dorothy Canfield Fisher. Harcourt, Brace

NONFICTION

1. *Diet and Health,* by Lulu Hunt Peters. Reilly & Lee

2. *The Life of Christ,* by Giovanni Papini. Harcourt, Brace

3. *The Boston Cooking School Cook Book; new ed.* by Fannie Farmer. Little, Brown

4. *Etiquette,* by Emily Post. Funk & Wagnalls

5. *Ariel,* by André Maurois. Appleton

6. *The Cross Word Puzzle Books,* by Prosper Buranelli and others. Simon & Schuster

7. *Mark Twain's Autobiography.* Harper

8. *Saint Joan,* by Bernard Shaw. Brentano

9. *The New Decalogue of Science,* by Albert E. Wiggam. Bobbs-Merrill

10. *The Americanization of Edward Bok,* by Edward Bok. Scribner

1925

FICTION

1. *Soundings,* by A. Hamilton Gibbs. Little, Brown

2. *The Constant Nymph,* by Margaret Kennedy. Doubleday, Page

3. *The Keeper of the Bees,* by Gene Stratton Porter. Doubleday, Page

4. *Glorious Apollo,* by E. Barrington. Dodd, Mead

5. *The Green Hat,* by Michael Arlen. Doran

6. *The Little French Girl,* by Anne Douglas Sedgwick. Houghton Mifflin

7. *Arrowsmith,* by Sinclair Lewis. Harcourt, Brace

8. *The Perennial Bachelor,* by Anne Parrish. Harper

9. *The Carolinian,* by Rafael Sabatini. Houghton Mifflin

10. *One Increasing Purpose,* by A. S. M. Hutchinson. Little, Brown

NONFICTION

1. *Diet and Health,* by Lulu Hunt Peters. Reilly & Lee

2. *The Boston Cooking School Cook Book; new ed.* by Fannie Farmer. Little, Brown

3. *When We Were Very Young,* by A. A. Milne. Dutton

4. *The Man Nobody Knows,* by Bruce Barton. Bobbs-Merrill

5. *The Life of Christ,* by Giovanni Papini. Harcourt, Brace

6. *Ariel,* by André Maurois. Appleton

7. *Twice Thirty,* by Edward Bok. Scribner

8. *Twenty-Five Years,* by Lord Grey. Stokes

9. *Anatole France Himself,* by J. J. Brousson. Lippincott

10. *The Cross Word Puzzle Books,* by Prosper Buranelli and others. 1st–4th series. Simon & Schuster

1926

FICTION

1. *The Private Life of Helen of Troy,* by John Erskine. Bobbs-Merrill

2. *Gentlemen Prefer Blondes,* by Anita Loos. Boni & Liveright

3. *Sorrell and Son,* by Warwick Deeping. Knopf

4. *The Hounds of Spring,* by Sylvia Thompson. Little, Brown

5. *Beau Sabreur,* by P. C. Wren. Stokes

6. *The Silver Spoon,* by John Galsworthy. Scribner

7. *Beau Geste,* by P. C. Wren. Stokes

8. *Show Boat,* by Edna Ferber. Doubleday, Page

9. *After Noon,* by Susan Ertz. Appleton

10. *The Blue Window,* by Temple Bailey. Penn Publishing Co.

NONFICTION

1. *The Man Nobody Knows,* by Bruce Barton. Bobbs-Merrill

2. *Why We Behave Like Human Beings,* by George A. Dorsey. Harper

3. *Diet and Health,* by Lulu Hunt Peters. Reilly & Lee

4. *Our Times, Vol. I,* by Mark Sullivan. Scribner

5. *The Boston Cooking School Cook Book; new ed.* by Fannie Farmer. Little, Brown

6. *Auction Bridge Complete,* by Milton C. Work. Winston

7. *The Book Nobody Knows,* by Bruce Barton. Bobbs-Merrill

8. *The Story of Philosophy,* by Will Durant. Simon & Schuster

9. *The Light of Faith,* by Edgar A. Guest. Reilly & Lee

10. *Jefferson and Hamilton,* by Claude G. Bowers. Houghton Mifflin

1927

FICTION

1. *Elmer Gantry,* by Sinclair Lewis. Harcourt, Brace
2. *The Plutocrat,* by Booth Tarkington. Doubleday, Page
3. *Doomsday,* by Warwick Deeping. Knopf
4. *Sorrell and Son,* by Warwick Deeping. Knopf
5. *Jalna,* by Mazo de la Roche. Little, Brown
6. *Lost Ecstasy,* by Mary Roberts Rinehart. Doran
7. *Twilight Sleep,* by Edith Wharton. Appleton
8. *Tomorrow Morning,* by Anne Parrish. Harper
9. *The Old Countess,* by Anne Douglas Sedgwick. Houghton Mifflin
10. *A Good Woman,* by Louis Bromfield. Stokes

NONFICTION

1. *The Story of Philosophy,* by Will Durant. Simon & Schuster
2. *Napoleon,* by Emil Ludwig. Boni & Liveright
3. *Revolt in the Desert,* by T. E. Lawrence. Doran
4. *Trader Horn, Vol. I,* by Alfred Aloysius Horn and Ethelreda Lewis. Simon & Schuster
5. *We,* by Charles A. Lindbergh. Putnam
6. *Ask Me Another,* by Julian Spafford and Lucien Esty. Viking Press
7. *The Royal Road to Romance,* by Richard Halliburton. Bobbs-Merrill
8. *The Glorious Adventure,* by Richard Halliburton. Bobbs-Merrill
9. *Why We Behave Like Human Beings,* by George A. Dorsey. Harper
10. *Mother India,* by Katherine Mayo. Harcourt, Brace

1928

FICTION

1. *The Bridge of San Luis Rey,* by Thornton Wilder. A. & C. Boni

2. *Wintersmoon,* by Hugh Walpole. Doubleday, Doran

3. *Swan Song,* by John Galsworthy. Scribner

4. *The Greene Murder Case,* by S. S. Van Dine. Scribner

5. *Bad Girl,* by Viña Delmar. Harcourt, Brace

6. *Claire Ambler,* by Booth Tarkington. Doubleday, Doran

7. *Old Pybus,* by Warwick Deeping. Knopf

8. *All Kneeling,* by Anne Parrish. Harper

9. *Jalna,* by Mazo de la Roche. Little, Brown

10. *The Strange Case of Miss Annie Spragg,* by Louis Bromfield. Stokes

NONFICTION

1. *Disraeli,* by André Maurois. Appleton

2. *Mother India,* by Katherine Mayo. Harcourt, Brace

3. *Trader Horn, Vol. I,* by Alfred Aloysius Horn and Ethelreda Lewis. Simon & Schuster

4. *Napoleon,* by Emil Ludwig. Liveright

5. *Strange Interlude,* by Eugene O'Neill. Liveright

6. *We,* by Charles A. Lindbergh. Putnam

7. *Count Luckner, the Sea Devil,* by Lowell Thomas. Doubleday, Doran

8. *Goethe,* by Emil Ludwig. Putnam

9. *Skyward,* by Richard E. Byrd. Putnam

10. *The Intelligent Woman's Gude to Socialism and Capitalism,* by George Bernard Shaw. Brentano

1929

FICTION

1. *All Quiet on the Western Front,* by Erich Maria Remarque. Little, Brown

2. *Dodsworth,* by Sinclair Lewis. Harcourt, Brace

3. *Dark Hester,* by Anne Douglas Sedgwick. Houghton Mifflin

4. *The Bishop Murder Case,* by S. S. Van Dine. Scribner

5. *Roper's Row,* by Warwick Deeping. Knopf

6. *Peder Victorious,* by O. E. Rölvaag. Harper

7. *Mamba's Daughters,* by DuBose Heyward. Doubleday, Doran

8. *The Galaxy,* by Susan Ertz. Appleton

9. *Scarlet Sister Mary,* by Julia Peterkin. Bobbs-Merrill

10. *Joseph and His Brethren,* by H. W. Freeman. Holt

NONFICTION

1. *The Art of Thinking,* by Ernest Dimnet. Simon & Schuster

2. *Henry the Eighth,* by Francis Hackett. Liveright

3. *The Cradle of the Deep,* by Joan Lowell. Simon & Schuster

4. *Elizabeth and Essex,* by Lytton Strachey. Harcourt, Brace

5. *The Specialist,* by Chic Sale. Specialist Publishing Co.

6. *A Preface to Morals,* by Walter Lippmann. Macmillan

7. *Believe It or Not,* by Robert L. Ripley. Simon & Schuster

8. *John Brown's Body,* by Stephen Vincent Benét. Doubleday, Doran

9. *The Tragic Era,* by Claude G. Bowers. Houghton Mifflin

10. *The Mansions of Philosophy,* by Will Durant. Simon & Schuster

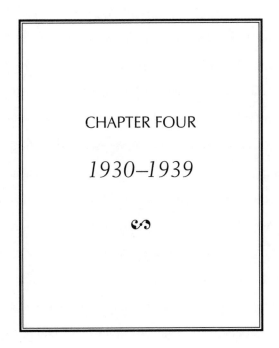

CHAPTER FOUR

1930–1939

cs

THE BIG NEWS IN PUBLISHING in the 1930s wasn't a book, but the fateful decision to make books returnable. As the economy collapsed and the Depression spread, publishers began to fear that the bookstores of America might go under before they did, if only because booksellers told them so in no uncertain terms. The heart of the problem was that you couldn't hope to sell a book to the public unless the stores stocked it in some quantity, and if the booksellers couldn't afford to order it, the publishers would be out of business. It was basically a question of "cash flow," though the phrase itself wasn't yet in use, but as the larger book publishers looked out over the scary landscape of a ruined economy, the only solution appeared to be the radical step of allowing booksellers to return to the publisher for credit their unsold books. A bookseller who had been persuaded to order fifty copies of a big novel and only sold twenty, could return his "overstock" of thirty to the publisher for credit. At first, this was thought of—on both sides—as an emergency measure, a way of keeping the stores afloat in the deepening storm of the Depression, but as the Depression wore on from year to year—American business would not really emerge from it until 1938 or 1939, when the huge rise in armament production began to warm up the economy—the measure became permanent. Even then, it was only in 1941, when the draft began to pull millions of young men into the armed forces, that unemployment definitely receded. Like so many emergency measures taken in the Depression, the returnability of books became institutionalized with time, so that even when prosperity returned, it continued, and is, indeed, still with us some seventy years later, as one of the basic business assumptions of the publishing industry. "Gone today, here tomorrow," as Bennett Cerf, the cofounder of Random House, put it, referring to Random House's list of books, and it is certainly true that book publishing was changed radically by the fact that books, unlike most manufactured products, could be returned by the retailer if they were unsold.

When I became an editor at Simon & Schuster, in 1958, it was the custom to take young editors out to the warehouse in New Jersey and show them a vast, gloomy space full of books gathering dust, millions of them it seemed. These were all "returns" from the booksellers and were meant as a warning to us to always remember that when we made a mistake, either by buying the wrong book, or by overprinting it through excessive optimism, there was a real consequence—the books came back, carton after carton of them, the homeward flow sometimes continuing for years. Publishers eventually adapted to the change—publishing books has always been a risky business, and this merely made it more so—but it had a profound effect on the publishing business, and would play a major role three or four decades later, when publishers began to seek safety by merging with each other, or selling their company to one of the big entertainment or media conglomerates, where the problem of returnability was unknown.

1930 certainly showed no radical change in the bestseller list. Edna Ferber was back at #1 (with *Cimarron*), Mary Roberts Rinehart continued to write a bestseller a year, the English writer J. B. Priestley hit the list for the first of many times, with *Angel Pavement,* and Thornton Wilder was back on the list. None of it seems very surprising, but there are signs of the future in *The Strange Death of President Harding,* a #2 bestseller that prefigures the later (and huge) successes of political writers like Bob Woodward and Carl Bernstein. Emil Ludwig's *Lincoln* and André Maurois's *Byron* showed that people were still reading about the past (so much less frightening than thinking about the present or the future), as did the continuation of Ernest Dimnet, Will Durant, and H. G. Wells on the list.

1931 brought a clutch of novels that would remain famous for decades, including Pearl S. Buck's *The Good Earth* (Mrs. Buck was also the first American woman to win the Nobel Prize for literature, in 1938), *Grand Hotel,* by Vicki Baum, and *Back Street,* by Fannie Hurst, all to be made into hugely successful movies. *Back Street* was—and remains—one of the great, enduring tearjerkers of all time, creating a whole genre that survives to this day.

Boners, at #4 on the nonfiction list, was another piece of merchandise and the direct ancestor of many successful imitations, which now have moved to television in the form of shows with the "funniest videos" of children or pets, or the worst "bloopers" of presidents. Equally noteworthy are two huge bestsellers about bridge, both by Ely Culbertson, marking the beginning of a new American craze, and perhaps the first, early sign of a return to what the late President Harding had referred to as "normalcy."

1932 saw the election of Franklin D. Roosevelt, and not one, but two novels by Pearl S. Buck on the list (at #1 and #3), as well as the debut on the list of Lloyd C. Douglas, a retired minister in his fifties whose novels on biblical themes would make him a bestseller for years to come, as well as A. J. Cronin, who would also go on for years.

In nonfiction, apart from the return of a bridge book by Ely Culbertson, there was Frederick Lewis Allen's *Only Yesterday,* a book about the twenties that was considered a classic for many years, and must still be in print today (if it's not, it ought to be), and a whole succession of books that indicate the degree to which the country's attention was beginning to turn toward Washington, including two by political columnist Drew Pearson. This represents a significant new trend. Hitherto, political books had been about the past, while the business of reporting on current events was left to the newspapers and, increasingly, to radio, but publishers were beginning to catch on to the fact that Washington was now where the action was, not the stock market or Hollywood, and began to cash in on books that were written and published quickly to take advantage of political events and news. Henceforth, book publishers kept an eye on the Washington scene or hired an editor whose special task it was to do so. Just as the bookstores had been obliged to learn the basics about modern merchandizing and would end up resembling in some ways the supermarket, book publishers, whose lists had traditionally been divided into fiction, nonfiction, history, and poetry, began to divide their lists into market-oriented categories, i.e., "health," "politics," "games and puzzles," "mysteries," with an editor in charge of each. The editor who could do it all was passing, to be replaced eventually by specialists, as publishers went through the same process of modernization that the larger urban booksellers had in the twenties.

1933 (the year of my birth) gave readers two novels by Lloyd C. Douglas, and introduced perhaps the most successful historical novel of the time, *Anthony Adverse,* by Hervey Allen, a book that not only gave rebirth to what was beginning to seem to many a "dead" category, the historical novel, but that also, by its sheer size, set a new standard for popular fiction. Henceforth, the "historical" would almost by definition be long, a tradition that would still be in force more than forty years later, when Larry McMurtry wrote *Lonesome Dove. Anthony Adverse* not only reawakened a whole market, but defined it: The historical novel would from now on be long, and readers who liked their "romantic fiction," say, at about three hundred pages, would expect their "historical fiction" to be six, seven, or even eight hundred densely printed pages long.

The year of my birth also saw the publication of a #1 nonfiction bestseller that set the trend for many more to come—*Life Begins at Forty,* by

Walter B. Pitkin, as well as President Roosevelt's own *Looking Forward,* reactivating a tradition begun by Woodrow Wilson of presidents reaching out to the reading classes with a book about what they planned to do in office. 1934 saw *Anthony Adverse* continue as #1 on the fiction list, but also introduced James Hilton's unforgettable *Good-Bye, Mr. Chips* and *Seven Gothic Tales* by Isak Dinesen. In nonfiction, Peter Fleming, the brother of Ian Fleming, who would later become the world-famous author of the James Bond novels, appeared on the list with a brilliant travel book, *Brazilian Adventure,* the first on the list of many fine travel books by understated, worldly British adventurers (a whole genre right there), as well as Romola Nijinsky's life of her husband, Alexander Woollcott's acerbic *While Rome Burns* (at #1) and *You Must Relax,* by Edmund Jacobson, again the forerunner of countless bestselling books advising Americans on how to sleep soundly, stop worrying, and gain control over their nerves.

It should be noted here that the bestseller list for 1934 demonstrates very clearly that Americans have always bought—and continue to buy—the same "mix" of books. Neither the fiction list nor the nonfiction list seems at all old-fashioned, or dated, including *Forty-two Years in the White House,* by Ike Hoover, which prefigures dozens of bestsellers by White House servants, ushers, and maids over the years, while the celebrity book is well represented by Alexander Woollcott and Romola Nijinsky, as are the limitations of that kind of publishing, since neither of them is a celebrity now (although Romola Nijinsky lived on to write me many letters about her book when I was a fledgling editor at Simon & Schuster).

1935 proved that Lloyd Douglas was in for the long haul, with *Green Light* at #1, and introduced to the bestseller list a major American talent with Thomas Wolfe's *Of Time and the River,* and was memorable for the publica-

tion of James Hilton's *Lost Horizon,* a book that has never lost its appeal, particularly for moviemakers. Repeaters included Edna Ferber, still going
strong, and Thornton Wilder. Franz Werfel's *The Forty Days of Musa Dagh*
had been a hugely successful European bestseller and became one here, too.
The nonfiction list included *Seven Pillars of Wisdom,* by T. E. Lawrence, a
huge, expensive, and fairly difficult book and a tribute to the public relations
legend that had been built up around the figure of Lawrence of Arabia, as
well as Clarence Day's timeless *Life with Father,* Anne Morrow Lindbergh's
North to the Orient, and Douglas Southall Freeman's monumental *R. E. Lee.*
Once again, this is a list of books that would probably be bestsellers today,
though it is worth noting that it took seventy years from the surrender at
Appomattox Court House for a big biography of Lee to hit the yearly bestseller list, demonstrating that the Civil War had at last become "history," as
the last of its surviving veterans died off, rather than still a partisan and sec-
tional subject.

1936 marked the publication of Margaret Mitchell's *Gone With the
Wind,* which was to be #1 for two years, and sold over a million copies in its
first year, setting records that the book still holds, and overwhelming the rest
of the fiction list which included *Drums Along the Mohawk,* Sinclair Lewis's
prescient *It Can't Happen Here,* and Aldous Huxley's brilliant *Eyeless in Gaza,*
as well as yet another novel by Mary Roberts Rinehart. It is worth noting,
once again, that Americans had a broad and curious interest in books. *Gone
With the Wind* was, admittedly, a phenomenon, but *Eyeless in Gaza* was literature, by a smart and thoughtful intellectual who made no compromises for
the reader, and did nothing to simplify his prose or his ideas. Those who think
of the bestseller list as representing the lowest common denominator have
never studied the bestseller list, and fail to understand that Americans want

to be challenged *and* entertained, and that there was room for "trash" and for "literature" on the list. The nonfiction list demonstrated the same kind of broad interest: a book by a successful doctor, a self-help "feel-good" inspirational book, John Gunther's *Inside Europe* (the first of many survey books by journalists and a sign of growing interest and alarm at what was happening on the other side of the Atlantic), and a journalist's memoirs.

1937 was a vintage year in fiction. Apart from the second year at #1 of *Gone With the Wind*, it included *Northwest Passage, Of Mice and Men, The Citadel,* and *The Rains Came,* all of them memorable and long-lived novels, as well as Virginia Woolf's *The Years,* and *Theatre* by W. Somerset Maugham. It also featured one of the great bestsellers of all time, on the nonfiction list, in the shape of Dale Carnegie's *How to Win Friends and Influence People.* 1938 would bring no great changes, except for two remarkable novels, *The Yearling,* by Marjorie Kinnan Rawlings (at #1), and *Rebecca,* by Daphne du Maurier. Once again, both of these novels would be bestsellers today, and indeed continue to sell.

The fiction list for 1939 includes *The Grapes of Wrath* (at #1), while *The Yearling* and *Rebecca* continue on the list. The nonfiction list includes Adolf Hitler's *Mein Kampf* and Antoine de St.-Exupéry's *Wind, Sand and Stars,* showing, if nothing else, an interest in the worst and best of Europe on the eve of war, and the aptly titled *Not Peace But a Sword,* by the famous journalist Vincent Sheean.

The are several things that this decade's bestseller list tell us, loud and clear. The first is that a remarkable number of important and serious novels do become big bestsellers—it ain't just Fannie Hurst, it's also Aldous Huxley, Steinbeck, Hemingway. The second is that Americans look toward books to explain to them what is happening, hence the success of John Gunther's books, or the sudden sale of *Mein Kampf*. The book has become the way we figure out what lies behind the news, and this remains true sixty years later, when the news is brought to us on television with interminable commentaries by learned pundits and authors—we still look to the book to explain, inform, and teach us. Finally, Americans still want to be amused, entertained, and improved. Joke books, puzzle books, self-improvement books, diet books, all represent part of the American national character, an endearing combination of good humor and dogged determination to improve and succeed that remains as true today as it was in 1939, and just as likely now and then to spawn bestsellers.

1930

FICTION

1. *Cimarron,* by Edna Ferber. Doubleday, Doran

2. *Exile,* by Warwick Deeping. Knopf

3. *The Woman of Andros,* by Thornton Wilder. A. & C. Boni

4. *Years of Grace,* by Margaret Ayer Barnes. Houghton Mifflin

5. *Angel Pavement,* by J. B. Priestley. Harper

6. *The Door,* by Mary Roberts Rinehart. Farrar & Rinehart

7. *Rogue Herries,* by Hugh Walpole. Doubleday, Doran

8. *Chances,* by A. Hamilton Gibbs. Little, Brown

9. *Young Man of Manhattan,* by Katharine Brush. Farrar & Rinehart

10. *Twenty-Four Hours,* by Louis Bromfield. Stokes

NONFICTION

1. *The Story of San Michele,* by Axel Munthe. Dutton

2. *The Strange Death of President Harding,* by Gaston B. Means and May Dixon Thacker. Guild Publishing Corp.

3. *Byron,* by André Maurois. Appleton

4. *The Adams Family,* by James Truslow Adams. Little, Brown

5. *Lone Cowboy,* by Will James. Scribner

6. *Lincoln,* by Emil Ludwig. Little, Brown

7. *The Story of Philosophy,* by Will Durant. Garden City Publishing Co.

8. *The Outline of History,* by H. G. Wells. Garden City Publishing Co.

9. *The Art of Thinking,* by Ernest Dimnet. Simon & Schuster

10. *The Rise of American Civilization,* by Charles and Mary Beard. Macmillan

1931

FICTION

1. *The Good Earth,* by Pearl S. Buck. John Day

2. *Shadows on the Rock,* by Willa Cather. Knopf

3. *A White Bird Flying,* by Bess Streeter Aldrich. Appleton

4. *Grand Hotel,* by Vicki Baum. Doubleday, Doran

5. *Years of Grace,* by Margaret Ayer Barnes. Houghton Mifflin

6. *The Road Back,* by Erich Maria Remarque. Little, Brown

7. *The Bridge of Desire,* by Warwick Deeping. McBride

8. *Back Street,* by Fannie Hurst. Cosmopolitan Book Co.

9. *Finch's Fortune,* by Mazo de la Roche. Little, Brown

10. *Maid in Waiting,* by John Galsworthy. Scribner

NONFICTION

1. *Education of a Princess,* by Grand Dutchess Marie. Viking Press

2. *The Story of San Michele,* by Axel Munthe. Dutton

3. *Washington Merry-Go-Round,* Anonymous (Drew Pearson and Robert S. Allen). Liveright

4. *Boners.* Viking Press

5. *Culbertson's Summary,* by Ely Culbertson. Bridge World

6. *Contract Bridge Blue Book,* by Ely Culbertson. Bridge World

7. *Fatal Interview,* by Edna St. Vincent Millay. Harper

8. *The Epic of America,* by James Truslow Adams. Little, Brown

9. *Mexico,* by Stuart Chase. Macmillan

10. *New Russia's Primer,* by M. Ilin. Houghton Mifflin

1932

FICTION

1. *The Good Earth,* by Pearl S. Buck. John Day

2. *The Fountain,* by Charles Morgan. Knopf

3. *Sons,* by Pearl S. Buck. John Day

4. *Magnolia Street,* by Louis Golding. Farrar & Rinehart

5. *The Sheltered Life,* by Ellen Glasgow. Doubleday, Doran

6. *Old Wine and New,* by Warwick Deeping. Knopf

7. *Mary's Neck,* by Booth Tarkington. Doubleday, Doran

8. *Magnificent Obsession,* by Lloyd C. Douglas. Willett, Clark

9. *Inheritance,* by Phyllis Bentley. Macmillan

10. *Three Loves,* by A. J. Cronin. Little, Brown

NONFICTION

1. *The Epic of America,* by James Truslow Adams. Little, Brown

2. *Only Yesterday,* by Frederick Lewis Allen. Harper

3. *A Fortune to Share,* by Vash Young. Bobbs-Merrill

4. *Culbertson's Summary,* by Ely Culbertson. Bridge World

5. *Van Loon's Geography,* by Hendrik Willem Van Loon. Simon & Schuster

6. *What We Live By,* by Ernest Dimnet. Simon & Schuster

7. *The March of Democracy,* by James Truslow Adams. Scribner

8. *Washington Merry-Go-Round,* Anonymous (Drew Pearson and Robert S. Allen). Liveright; Blue Ribbon Books

9. *The Story of My Life,* by Clarence Darrow. Scribner

10. *More Merry-Go-Round,* Anonymous (Drew Pearson and Robert S. Allen). Liveright

1933

FICTION

1. *Anthony Adverse,* by Hervey Allen. Farrar & Rinehart

2. *As the Earth Turns,* by Gladys Hasty Carroll. Macmillan

3. *Ann Vickers,* by Sinclair Lewis. Doubleday, Doran

4. *Magnificent Obsession,* by Lloyd C. Douglas. Willett, Clark

5. *One More River,* by John Galsworthy. Scribner

6. *Forgive Us Our Trespasses,* by Lloyd C. Douglas. Houghton Mifflin

7. *The Master of Jalna,* by Mazo de la Roche. Little, Brown

8. *Miss Bishop,* by Bess Streeter Aldrich. Appleton-Century

9. *The Farm,* by Louis Bromfield. Harper

10. *Little Man, Now What?* by Hans Fallada. Simon & Schuster

NONFICTION

1. *Life Begins at Forty,* by Walter B. Pitkin. Whittlesey House

2. *Marie Antoinette,* by Stefan Zweig. Viking Press

3. *British Agent,* by R. H. Bruce Lockhart. Putnam

4. *100,000,000 Guinea Pigs,* by Arthur Kallet and F. J. Schlink. Vanguard Press

5. *The House of Exile,* by Nora Waln. Little, Brown

6. *Van Loon's Geography,* by Hendrik Willem Van Loon. Simon & Schuster

7. *Looking Forward,* by Franklin D. Roosevelt. John Day

8. *Contract Bridge Blue Book of 1933,* by Eli Culbertson. Bridge World

9. *The Arches of the Years,* by Halliday Sutherland. Morrow

10. *The March of Democracy, Vol. II,* by James Truslow Adams. Scribner

1934

FICTION

1. *Anthony Adverse,* by Hervey Allen. Farrar & Rinehart

2. *Lamb in His Bosom,* by Caroline Miller. Harper

3. *So Red the Rose,* by Stark Young. Scribner

4. *Good-Bye, Mr. Chips,* by James Hilton. Little, Brown

5. *Within This Present,* by Margaret Ayer Barnes. Houghton Mifflin

6. *Work of Art,* by Sinclair Lewis. Doubleday, Doran

7. *Private Worlds,* by Phyllis Bottome. Houghton Mifflin

8. *Mary Peters,* by Mary Ellen Chase. Macmillan

9. *Oil for the Lamps of China,* by Alice Tisdale Hobart. Bobbs-Merrill

10. *Seven Gothic Tales,* by Isak Dinesen. Smith & Haas

NONFICTION

1. *While Rome Burns,* by Alexander Woollcott. Viking Press

2. *Life Begins at Forty,* by Walter B. Pitkin. Whittlesey House

3. *Nijinsky,* by Romola Nijinsky. Simon & Schuster

4. *100,000,000 Guinea Pigs,* by Arthur Kallet and F. J. Schlink. Vanguard Press

5. *The Native's Return,* by Louis Adamic. Harper

6. *Stars Fell on Alabama,* by Carl Carmer. Farrar & Rinehart

7. *Brazilian Adventure,* by Peter Fleming. Scribner

8. *Forty-two Years in the White House,* by Ike Hoover. Houghton Mifflin

9. *You Must Relax,* by Edmund Jacobson. Whittlesey House

10. *The Life of Our Lord,* by Charles Dickens. Simon & Schuster

1935

FICTION

1. *Green Light,* by Lloyd C. Douglas. Houghton Mifflin

2. *Vein of Iron,* by Ellen Glasgow. Harcourt, Brace

3. *Of Time and the River,* by Thomas Wolfe. Scribner

4. *Time Out of Mind,* by Rachel Field. Macmillan

5. *Good-Bye, Mr. Chips,* by James Hilton. Little, Brown

6. *The Forty Days of Musa Dagh,* by Franz Werfel. Viking Press

7. *Heaven's My Destination,* by Thornton Wilder. Harper

8. *Lost Horizon,* by James Hilton. Morrow

9. *Come and Get It,* by Edna Ferber. Doubleday, Doran

10. *Europa,* by Robert Briffault. Scribner

NONFICTION

1. *North to the Orient,* by Anne Morrow Lindbergh. Harcourt, Brace

2. *While Rome Burns,* by Alexander Woollcott. Viking Press

3. *Life with Father,* by Clarence Day. Knopf

4. *Personal History,* by Vincent Sheean. Doubleday, Doran

5. *Seven Pillars of Wisdom,* by T. E. Lawrence. Doubleday, Doran

6. *Francis the First,* by Francis Hackett. Doubleday, Doran

7. *Mary Queen of Scotland and the Isles,* by Stefan Zweig. Viking Press

8. *Rats, Lice and History,* by Hans Zinsser. Little, Brown

9. *R. E. Lee,* by Douglas Southall Freeman. Scribner

10. *Skin Deep,* by M. C. Phillips. Vanguard Press

1936

FICTION

1. *Gone With the Wind,* by Margaret Mitchell. Macmillan

2. *The Last Puritan,* by George Santayana. Scribner

3. *Sparkenbroke,* by Charles Morgan. Macmillan

4. *Drums Along the Mohawk,* by Walter D. Edmonds. Little, Brown

5. *It Can't Happen Here,* by Sinclair Lewis. Doubleday, Doran

6. *White Banners,* by Lloyd C. Douglas. Houghton Mifflin

7. *The Hurricane,* by Charles Nordhoff and James Norman Hall. Little, Brown

8. *The Thinking Reed,* by Rebecca West. Viking Press

9. *The Doctor,* by Mary Roberts Rinehart. Farrar & Rinehart

10. *Eyeless in Gaza,* by Aldous Huxley. Harper

NONFICTION

1. *Man the Unknown,* by Alexis Carrel. Harper

2. *Wake Up and Live!* by Dorothea Brande. Simon & Schuster

3. *The Way of a Transgressor,* by Negley Farson. Harcourt, Brace

4. *Around the World in Eleven Years,* by Patience, Richard, and Johnny Abbe. Stokes

5. *North to the Orient,* by Anne Morrow Lindbergh. Harcourt, Brace

6. *An American Doctor's Odyssey,* by Victor Heiser. Norton

7. *Inside Europe,* by John Gunther. Harper

8. *Live Alone and Like It,* by Marjorie Hillis. Bobbs-Merrill

9. *Life with Father,* by Clarence Day. Knopf

10. *I Write As I Please,* by Walter Duranty. Simon & Schuster

1937

FICTION

1. *Gone With the Wind,* by Margaret Mitchell. Macmillan

2. *Northwest Passage,* by Kenneth Roberts. Doubleday, Doran

3. *The Citadel,* by A. J. Cronin. Little, Brown

4. *And So—Victoria,* by Vaughan Wilkins. Macmillan

5. *Drums Along the Mohawk,* by Walter D. Edmonds. Little, Brown

6. *The Years,* by Virginia Woolf. Harcourt, Brace

7. *Theatre,* by W. Somerset Maugham. Doubleday, Doran

8. *Of Mice and Men,* by John Steinbeck. Covici, Friede

9. *The Rains Came,* by Louis Bromfield. Harper

10. *We Are Not Alone,* by James Hilton. Little, Brown

NONFICTION

1. *How to Win Friends and Influence People,* by Dale Carnegie. Simon & Schuster

2. *An American Doctor's Odyssey,* by Victor Heiser. Norton

3. *The Return to Religion,* by Henry C. Link. Macmillan

4. *The Arts,* by Hendrik Willem Van Loon. Simon & Schuster

5. *Orchids on Your Budget,* by Marjorie Hillis. Bobbs-Merrill

6. *Present Indicative,* by Noel Coward. Doubleday, Doran

7. *Mathematics for the Million,* by Lancelot Hogben. Norton

8. *Life with Mother,* by Clarence Day. Knopf

9. *The Nile,* by Emil Ludwig. Viking Press

10. *The Flowering of New England,* by Van Wyck Brooks. Dutton

1938

FICTION

1. *The Yearling,* by Marjorie Kinnan Rawlings. Scribner

2. *The Citadel,* by A. J. Cronin. Little, Brown

3. *My Son, My Son!* by Howard Spring. Viking Press

4. *Rebecca,* by Daphne du Maurier. Doubleday, Doran

5. *Northwest Passage,* by Kenneth Roberts. Doubleday, Doran

6. *All This, and Heaven Too,* by Rachel Field. Macmillan

7. *The Rains Came,* by Louis Bromfield. Harper

8. *And Tell of Time,* by Laura Krey. Houghton Mifflin

9. *The Mortal Storm,* by Phyllis Bottome. Little, Brown

10. *Action at Aquila,* by Hervey Allen. Farrar & Rinehart

NONFICTION

1. *The Importance of Living,* by Lin Yutang. John Day

2. *With Malice Toward Some,* by Margaret Halsey. Simon & Schuster

3. *Madame Curie,* by Eve Curie. Doubleday, Doran

4. *Listen! the Wind,* by Anne Morrow Lindbergh. Harcourt, Brace

5. *The Horse and Buggy Doctor,* by Arthur E. Hertzler. Harper

6. *How to Win Friends and Influence People,* by Dale Carnegie. Simon & Schuster

7. *Benjamin Franklin,* by Carl Van Doren. Viking Press

8. *I'm a Stranger Here Myself,* by Ogden Nash. Little, Brown

9. *Alone,* by Richard E. Byrd. Putnam

10. *Fanny Kemble,* by Margaret Armstrong. Macmillan

1939

FICTION

1. *The Grapes of Wrath,* by John Steinbeck. Viking Press

2. *All This, and Heaven Too,* by Rachel Field. Macmillan

3. *Rebecca,* by Daphne du Maurier. Doubleday, Doran

4. *Wickford Point,* by John P. Marquand. Little, Brown

5. *Escape,* by Ethel Vance. Little, Brown

6. *Disputed Passage,* by Lloyd C. Douglas. Houghton Mifflin

7. *The Yearling,* by Marjorie Kinnan Rawlings. Scribner

8. *The Tree of Liberty,* by Elizabeth Page. Farrar & Rinehart

9. *The Nazarene,* by Sholem Asch. Putnam

10. *Kitty Foyle,* by Christopher Morley. Lippincott

NONFICTION

1. *Days of Our Years,* by Pierre van Paassen. Hillman-Curl

2. *Reaching for the Stars,* by Nora Waln. Little, Brown

3. *Inside Asia,* by John Gunther. Harper

4. *Autobiography with Letters,* by William Lyon Phelps. Oxford University Press

5. *Country Lawyer,* by Bellamy Partridge. Whittlesey House

6. *Wind, Sand and Stars,* by Antoine de St.-Exupéry. Reynal & Hitchcock

7. *Mein Kampf,* by Adolf Hitler. Reynal & Hitchcock

8. *A Peculiar Treasure,* by Edna Ferber. Doubleday, Doran

9. *Not Peace But a Sword,* by Vincent Sheean. Doubleday, Doran

10. *Listen! the Wind,* by Anne Morrow Lindbergh. Harcourt, Brace

CHAPTER FIVE

1940–1949

ఴ

A WORD ABOUT THE BOOK BUSINESS before World War Two. The mass-market paperback business was still in its infancy. The war decade to come would change that. Pocket Books had been founded in the thirties, to sell books at twenty-five cents a copy. These paperbacks were distributed by magazine wholesalers to drugstores, candy stands, and news stores, but bookstores as such didn't carry them, or even acknowledge, for the most part, their existence. Pocket Books soon had plenty of rivals in the paperback business, which was already fiercely competitive and fast growing, but it would take the war, when millions of men had time on their hands to read, in training camps or on troop ships, and millions of women were at home, waiting for their return, to make the mass-market business really take off, and indeed, for a time, to achieve dominance over the hardcover book business.

Successful mass-market paperback titles sold in the millions of copies, dwarfing the numbers sold in hardcover by conventional booksellers (Dr. Spock's *Baby and Child Care* has sold close to 25 million copies in mass-market paperback, over the years), though there would not be a paperback bestseller list until 1955. By the end of the forties, perhaps even by the mid- to late-thirties, the hardcover bestseller only presented part of the story, therefore. There were books, like the sexy, hardboiled detective novels of Mickey Spillane, which did not appear on the hardcover lists at all, but would sell 5 million and more in "mass market." There were books that were major bestsellers in hardcover, and went on to become huge bestsellers in mass market, and books that sold a lot of copies in hardcover and never appeared in mass-market editions. In short, after the Second World War, there would be two different book markets: the "mass" market of paperback publishing, which mostly sold in outlets other than bookstores, and the conventional hardcover book business, centered on the bookstore, which, despite the growing help of the book clubs, sold fewer books, but at much higher prices.

It must be borne in mind, therefore, that when looking at the bestseller list from the 1940s on, we are only getting *part* of the story about book sales. Not that the market for hardcover books was necessarily small. Alice Payne Hackett puts the total hardcover sale of the *Better Homes and Gardens Cookbook* at over 18 million copies. That's a lot of books. Lloyd C. Douglas's *The Robe* would sell over 3 million copies, and several of the Dr. Seuss books would reach nearly 6 million copies in hardcover. Still, the average hardcover bestseller sold in numbers far smaller than these—more typically, Anne Morrow Lindbergh's *North to the Orient* became the #1 bestseller of 1935 with a sale of 185,000 copies, and to this day, in the beginning of a new century, a sale of 250,000 to 350,000 copies gives a book a fair crack at the very top of the list, unless there's some long-running phenomenon up there ahead of it, and those numbers could perhaps be doubled for the fiction list.

It is important to keep the list in perspective—for a hardcover book to reach six figures in sales is a considerable achievement (my own #1 hardcover bestseller, *Power!*, reached the top spot with about 350,000 in print, and after returns, probably had a net sale of around 200,000); Daphne du Maurier's *Rebecca* was a big bestseller when it was published in 1939, and reached #3 on the list, yet probably had a net sale of under 200,000 copies, but would go on to a long life in cheaper mass-market form, though still far behind such landmark mass-market fiction bestsellers as *The Godfather* (nearly 12 million), *Peyton Place* (over 10 million), *Jaws* (over 9 million), and *God's Little Acre* (over 8 million).

In 1940 Europe had been at war for a year, and the bestseller list for the year includes that memorably effective and subtle piece of propaganda for the British way of life, *Mrs. Miniver,* by Jan Struther, at #3, in a year that also included *How Green Was My Valley,* by Richard Llewellyn, Ernest Hemingway's *For Whom the Bell Tolls,* and Sholem Asch's *The Nazarene.* This is not a list to take lightly, especially since *The Grapes of Wrath* is still on it, too, and belies the accusation that only fluff makes the list.

In nonfiction, there was a trend toward politics with *Country Squire in the White House* (a portrait of FDR) and Joseph W. Alsop's *American White Paper,* but the biggest bestseller of the year was Osa Johnson's *I Married Adventure,* about the author's travels with her explorer husband, which sold (according to the invaluable Ms. Hackett) 288,000 copies; Mortimer Adler's *How to Read a Book,* which is still in print; and *A Smattering of Ignorance,* by Oscar Levant, the pianist and Hollywood wit. Once again, the mix is very contemporary: a book about the president, a survey of the country by a noted journalist and pundit (soon to become a national institution), a literary self-help book, and a book of exotic travel and adventure by a celebrity (Osa Johnson and her husband made hugely successful movies of their adventures and lectured relentlessly). The same mix of books might easily appear on the bestseller list today, and frequently does. It is also worth noting that long before television reached the home, all of these people would have made terrific guests on any TV talk show—indeed some of them lived on to appear on TV. Levant was certainly around to take advantage of TV, while Adler and Alsop lived on to become celebrity pundits. In short, though this list is sixty years old, it presents a very accurate summary of the kind of book, that, even today, is likely to have a crack at the nonfiction bestseller, and also demonstrates that before the "TV talk show" was even imagined, authors with the right mix of celebrity, personal salesmanship, and popular ideas were writing and promoting bestsellers very effectively. Television would shortly add a new dimension to this, but it did not, by itself, invent the kind of book and author that Americans wanted to read in large numbers. It is important to keep this in mind, since there is a tendency among intellectual purists to blame what they see as the decline of publishing standards on television, or on the book publishers' determination to exploit television to sell books. The bestseller list presents a different picture. Television would merely make it easier to promote a book—instead of having to send Osa Johnson and her husband around the country with their 16mm movie projector and their slides to lecture and sign books, you could put them on *The Today Show* right there in New York City, or fly them out to L.A. to appear on *The Tonight Show* with Johnny Carson or *The Merv Griffin Show* (then the big late-night talk shows), and reach millions of people, but the pitch, the product, and the sales tools were the same; it would merely take ten days or so to accomplish what had once taken months of expensive travel time. And even today, in the digital world, the first question any publisher asks an author is will he (or she) go and sign books in bookstores and does he (or she) give lectures? In the end, nothing beats pressing the flesh and signing the book—the face-to-face encounter, either in the bookstore or after the lecture (where, hopefully, a local bookseller will have set up a table and a cash register to sell the author's book). This is the basic building block of selling books, even today, sixty years later, and Osa Johnson with her slide show and her 16mm movies was good enough at it that older people could still remember her descent on places like Shaker Heights or Bloomington when I came into book publishing in 1958, and probably didn't buy another book about Africa until the advent of Elsa the lion, in *Born Free*. When I was a kid, I remember reading Osa Johnson—the beginning of a lifelong fascination with East Africa—and also Zane Grey's wonderful nonfiction books on big-game fishing, and while

Like That pretty much set the tone—six out of ten books were about the war or politics, one of which, St.-Exupéry's *Flight to Arras,* is a classic, and at least four of which were made into movies (though all those involved in the making of *Mission to Moscow* ended up being grilled by the House Un-American Activities Committee after the war). 1943 would see eight out of ten nonfiction books on the list relating to the war or war politics, including Republican presidential candidate Wendell L. Willkie's *One World,* which was sold in hardcover and paperback editions simultaneously, to the tune of over 1,500,000 copies, and at #1, prefiguring the postwar era, John Roy Carlson's *Under Cover,* an exposé of subversive activity in the United States. Fiction in 1942 and 1943 included novels that would be read for decades to come: *The Song of Bernadette, The Robe, Kings Row, The Keys of the Kingdom, A Tree Grows in Brooklyn,* and *The Human Comedy,* all of which would be made into movies.

Attentive fiction readers will also notice that while murder mysteries, historical novels, and romances inevitably take up a number of "slots" on the fiction list, most of the really big fiction bestsellers over the years are what publishers call "big novels," which is to say ambitious novels with a big theme, a big scope, larger-than-life-size characters, whether written at the "popular" level, like *The Robe,* or at the literary level, like *For Whom the Bell Tolls.* "Category" fiction certainly sells, but it is the big novel that publishers really look for, and—though perhaps not always consciously—readers, too. *The Song of Bernadette, Kings Row, The Keys of the Kingdom,* and Pearl S. Buck's *Dragon Seed* are all, in different ways, big novels, i.e., big in length, big in concept, with a big, central moral conflict, trying hard to be solid, serious, challenging, as well as entertaining. True, time, the ultimate judge of long-term bestsellerdom, has not been kind to them, nor even to Hemingway—Pearl S. Buck is seldom read today, *Song of Bernadette* hardly remembered, *Kings Row* and *Keys of the Kingdom* only by older readers—still, all of them were, as it were, considered "serious contenders" in their day.

The big novel could, of course, include romance; it might be "historical," but it first of all required a big *subject,* and a strong point of view about that subject. Very often it was sociological (Sinclair Lewis), or attempted to re-create and explain a whole alien culture (Pearl S. Buck on China, or, later, Norman Mailer on Egypt in *Ancient Evenings*), or sometimes it was a combination of ideology and reporting (*For Whom the Bell Tolls,* for example, but also, on a higher plane, *War and Peace*), but like a good French meal, it should leave the reader stuffed, satisfied, overwhelmed, in any event not hungry for more.

War, of course, was a major subject for such novels, though they tended to follow the war, not to get written during it, but whatever the subject, it was one of the two major categories of bestselling fiction, the big novel being trumped, as it were, only by that equally elusive phenomenon, "The Great American Novel," of which *Moby-Dick* is held to be the first example, except in the eyes of confirmed James Fennimore Cooper fans. The Great American Novel was best exemplified in the thirties by Thomas Wolfe—and in its contemporary form implied a big, long, multigenerational novel that at once illuminated and explained American life and was written by an American. It could not be "historical"; it had to have the kind of complex prose style that Theodore Dreiser, for example, always strived for; it had to be set firmly in the United States (which excluded most of the work of Hemingway and some of Fitzgerald's); and it had to make, or be thought by critics to have made, a serious, and perhaps even solemn, statement about American values.

Sinclair Lewis, Dreiser, Wolfe, and Steinbeck battled it out for supremacy in this area over the thirties and forties, though Dreiser seemed to many readers too heavy going, while Lewis was a bit of a hack (too many bestsellers written too quickly) and too many of Steinbeck's characters were quaint, fey, or out of the mainstream, which left Wolfe as the winner by default. In any case, these two categories—the big novel and the Great American Novel—tend to provide at least half of the fiction bestsellers and provide the all-important touchstone against which the importance and seriousness of a bestseller tends to be judged.

This should be a lesson for all of those who think that a novel has to be sexy or lowbrow to hit the list. American readers are certainly open to sexy books (sexy for their time, that is—one generation's sexy novel seems pale stuff to the next), but on the whole they tend to take seriously authors who take themselves seriously, and believe, in some inner core of their being, that a book ought to teach them something, or open their eyes to seeing something, even themselves, in a new way. Sinclair Lewis certainly did that, which perhaps explains why he stayed popular for so long, and it is in his wake that some of the most successful bestselling fiction writers of our own day have followed, among them Tom Wolfe.

1944 brought no surprises to the bestseller list in terms of fiction—it was mostly a continuation of 1943—except for the biggest "bodice ripper" of the twentieth century, and the first book to become a bestseller because it was considered outrageously sexy. Kathleen Winsor's *Forever Amber*—which was, literally, banned in Boston—opened the door for later writers like Grace Metalious and Jacqueline Susann, though it is worth noting that although it was in its second year on the list, *The Robe* outsold it, thus exemplifying the bipolar sexual mentality of the American reader, which could absorb both a pious religious epic and a bawdy Restoration historical novel at the same time. Half of the nonfiction list was either about war or politics—hardly surprising in the year of D-Day and a presidential election—but is notable for Bob Hope's first appearance on the list, for Gene Fowler's biography of John Barrymore, *Good Night, Sweet Prince* (a book that bowled me over when I read it at the age of thirteen), and for Margaret Landon's *Anna and the King of Siam,* which would soon become the musical, and later the movie, *The King and I.*

The year of victory produced no surprises in fiction, except for the first of Irving Stone's many bestsellers, and the fact that *Forever Amber* went to #1, but was remarkable for the appearance on the nonfiction list of *Black Boy,* by Richard Wright, the first of a string of autobiographical books by black men that brought home to white readers their authors' discomfort and anger with American life.

This, too, set a pattern. One of the things that the bestseller list certainly demonstrates is that American readers have been, since the 1940s, increasingly willing to be challenged and even attacked. They might not have been eager to accept these challenges in person—schools were still segregated in the South on principle, and in the North by neighborhood—but they were willing to buy and read books that criticized the status quo. Far from being complacent and self-satisfied, book buyers were willing, indeed eager, for the literature of protest and of complaint—something that would be borne out during the next ten years by the enormous success of *Gentleman's Agreement* (which tackled anti-Semitism in America in a popular novel) in 1947 and *The Man in the Gray Flannel Suit* (which took on advertising, business success, and the white upper-middle-class lifestyle, where most of the readers who bought bestselling books were to be found) in 1955. Escapism sold books, to be sure, but not nearly as many as were sold by exposing America's flaws and making the average American reader (and book club member) look closely at his or her most cherished social assumptions. Americans might not be eager to accept integration, feminism, homosexuality, juvenile delinquency, and the drug culture—or to shoulder the blame for the existence of these problems—but they were certainly willing to *read* about them, as the next five decades would prove. Indeed, 1946 brought two novels to the list that would make uncomfortable reading for many even today, *The Snake Pit,* a searing book about mental institutions, and *The Hucksters,* a savage indictment of the advertising industry. The year also brought, on the nonfiction list, the first of many bestselling books about the Cold War, *I Chose Freedom,* by Victor Kravchenko, signifying the beginning of a whole new historical era, and a whole new bestselling genre. There had been fiction bestsellers about espionage before, including books by Conrad, John Buchan, Graham Greene, and Eric Ambler, but it remained a kind of minor genre, as compared to the detective novel, and dominated by British writers. The Cold War–espionage novel, like the Cold War–nonfiction confessional book, would become a major staple of book publishing, and like the Cold War itself, would eventually be dominated by Americans.

1947 was made remarkable by the third year on the list of Betty MacDonald's *The Egg and I,* a book that had me in stitches when I first read it in 1948, on the way across the Atlantic to school in Switzerland, and remains the funniest of the "back to the simple life in the country" books that followed it. It created a whole new genre, of hapless city folk confronting country life, that would eventually include *Mr. Blandings Builds His Dream House* and my own *Country Matters,* and signify a whole new wave of American migration, for as the poor moved to the cities in the wake of the war, the well-to-do moved away from them—suburbia and exurbia were born, and by the end of the decade the bookstores, too, would be moving from the city streets to places that had once been cow pastures.

1948 is memorable for the publication of two novels: Norman Mailer's *The Naked and the Dead* and Irwin Shaw's *The Young Lions*. Here, attention should be paid. In the first place this was a major step, in that two hugely successful novels on the bestseller list were written by American Jews, whereas the fiction list had hitherto been dominated by Europeans, Englishmen, and WASPs. Secondly, both these books were sensational. The fiction to come out of World War One had mostly been written by officers, but Shaw and Mailer had been enlisted men, and their books reflected a view of the war in which the real enemy was not the Japanese or the Germans, but their own officers and the generals who ran the war.

Curiously, this had been the underlying theme of most British writing after World War One, in which the enemy was not the Germans, but the British generals who had persisted in four years of bloodletting on the Western Front with no discernible strategy or gain. In England, post-1918, there were two different and opposed views of the war, one that it was a heroic but senseless tragedy, the other that it was a stupid and avoidable one. Sorrow for the more than a million British dead—and respect for their heroism, however wasteful—mixed with rage at the stupidity of the generals that sent them out of the trenches and into the barbed wire against machine-gun fire and massed artillery (on the first *day* of the Battle of the Somme in 1916 alone, the British Army took 60,000 casualties in an area the size of Central Park, for almost no meaningful gain in ground). This profound revulsion ran deep in British literature, and must be taken into account in the thirties, when Baldwin hesitated to rearm and Chamberlain sought to appease Hitler.

The British had experienced the horrors of world war, and would do almost anything to avoid another one.

By contrast, after World War Two, confronted with the loss of empire, British writing, fiction and nonfiction, became self-congratulatory and hero-ic, a whole genre springing up to remind the British, from generation to gen-eration, of their own courage, exemplified by the huge sale of the six volumes of Winston Churchill's *The Second World War.* American fiction writers, however, wrote about the Second World War in the same vein as the British had after World War One. It was war itself that was the enemy, as well as the officers, generals, and politicians on our side. Mailer and Shaw were soon eclipsed by James Jones, who, at his best, was easier (and tougher) reading, but the antiwar war novel became a fixture in American life, gaining new ground with the publication of Joseph Heller's *Catch-22,* and later with a new generation's writing against the Vietnam War. To a great extent, it was the writing of novelists like Mailer and Shaw and Jones that soured Americans on World War Two, even as they were celebrating its victory, and led them to question the whole validity of war—doubts that would not affect public policy until the mid-1960s, but whose beginning can be traced, in direct line, to the two bestselling novels of 1948.

1949 brought to the fiction list a whole roster of names that would be famous: John O'Hara, John P. Marquand, Frances Parkinson Keyes, Thomas B. Costain, and Frank Yerby. As for the nonfiction list, the presence of *three* bestsellers about canasta, the new card game that was sweeping the country and replacing bridge, is proof enough that despite the war novels and the Cold War, Americans were back at peace again.

1940

—•—

FICTION

1. *How Green Was My Valley,* by Richard Llewellyn. Macmillan

2. *Kitty Foyle,* by Christopher Morley. Lippincott

3. *Mrs. Miniver,* by Jan Struther. Harcourt, Brace

4. *For Whom the Bell Tolls,* by Ernest Hemingway. Scribner

5. *The Nazarene,* by Sholem Asch. Putnam

6. *Stars on the Sea,* by F. van Wyck Mason. Lippincott

7. *Oliver Wiswell,* by Kenneth Roberts. Doubleday, Doran

8. *The Grapes of Wrath,* by John Steinbeck. Viking Press

9. *Night in Bombay,* by Louis Bromfield. Harper

10. *The Family,* by Nina Federova. Little, Brown

NONFICTION

1. *I Married Adventure,* by Osa Johnson. Lippincott

2. *How to Read a Book,* by Mortimer Adler. Simon & Schuster

3. *A Smattering of Ignorance,* by Oscar Levant. Doubleday, Doran

4. *Country Squire in the White House,* by John T. Flynn. Doubleday, Doran

5. *Land Below the Wind,* by Agnes Newton Keith. Little, Brown

6. *American White Paper,* by Joseph W. Alsop Jr. and Robert Kintnor.
   Simon & Schuster

7. *New England: Indian Summer,* by Van Wyck Brooks. Dutton

8. *As I Remember Him,* by Hans Zinsser. Little, Brown

9. *Days of Our Years,* by Pierre van Paassen. Dial Press

10. *Bet It's a Boy,* by Betty B. Blunt. Stephen Daye Press

1941

FICTION

1. *The Keys of the Kingdom,* by A. J. Cronin. Little, Brown

2. *Random Harvest,* by James Hilton. Little, Brown

3. *This Above All,* by Eric Knight. Harper

4. *The Sun Is My Undoing,* by Marguerite Steen. Viking Press

5. *For Whom the Bell Tolls,* by Ernest Hemingway. Scribner

6. *Oliver Wiswell,* by Kenneth Roberts. Doubleday, Doran

7. *H. M. Pulham, Esquire,* by John P. Marquand. Little, Brown

8. *Mr. and Mrs. Cugat,* by Isabel Scott Rorick. Houghton Mifflin

9. *Saratoga Trunk,* by Edna Ferber. Doubleday, Doran

10. *Windswept,* by Mary Ellen Chase. Macmillan

NONFICTION

1. *Berlin Diary,* by William L. Shirer. Knopf

2. *The White Cliffs,* by Alice Duer Miller. Coward-McCann

3. *Out of the Night,* by Jan Valtin. Alliance Book Corp.

4. *Inside Latin America,* by John Gunther. Harper

5. *Blood, Sweat and Tears,* by Winston S. Churchill. Putnam

6. *You Can't Do Business with Hitler,* by Douglas Miller. Little, Brown

7. *Reading I've Liked,* ed. by Clifton Fadiman. Simon & Schuster

8. *Reveille in Washington,* by Margaret Leech. Harper

9. *Exit Laughing,* by Irvin S. Cobb. Bobbs-Merrill

10. *My Sister and I,* by Dirk van der Heide. Harcourt, Brace

1942

FICTION

1. *The Song of Bernadette,* by Franz Werfel. Viking Press

2. *The Moon Is Down,* by John Steinbeck. Viking Press

3. *Dragon Seed,* by Pearl S. Buck. John Day

4. *And Now Tomorrow,* by Rachel Field. Macmillan

5. *Drivin' Woman,* by Elizabeth Pickett. Macmillan

6. *Windswept,* by Mary Ellen Chase. Macmillan

7. *The Robe,* by Lloyd C. Douglas. Houghton Mifflin

8. *The Sun Is My Undoing,* by Marguerite Steen. Viking Press

9. *Kings Row,* by Henry Bellamann. Simon & Schuster

10. *The Keys of the Kingdom,* by A. J. Cronin. Little, Brown

NONFICTION

1. *See Here, Private Hargrove,* by Marion Hargrove. Holt

2. *Mission to Moscow,* by Joseph E. Davies. Simon & Schuster

3. *The Last Time I Saw Paris,* by Elliot Paul. Random House

4. *Cross Creek,* by Marjorie Kinnan Rawlings. Scribner

5. *Victory Through Air Power,* by Major Alexander P. de Seversky.
   Simon & Schuster

6. *Past Imperfect,* by Ilka Chase. Doubleday, Chase

7. *They Were Expendable,* by W. L. White. Harcourt, Brace

8. *Flight to Arras,* by Antoine de St.-Exupéry. Reynal & Hitchcock

9. *Washington Is Like That,* by W. M. Kiplinger. Harper

10. *Inside Latin America,* by John Gunther. Harper

1943

FICTION

1. *The Robe,* by Lloyd C. Douglas. Houghton Mifflin

2. *The Valley of Decision,* by Marcia Davenport. Scribner

3. *So Little Time,* by John P. Marquand. Little, Brown

4. *A Tree Grows in Brooklyn,* by Betty Smith. Harper

5. *The Human Comedy,* by William Saroyan. Harcourt, Brace

6. *Mrs. Parkington,* by Louis Bromfield. Harper

7. *The Apostle,* by Sholem Asch. Putnam

8. *Hungry Hill,* by Daphne du Maurier. Doubleday, Doran

9. *The Forest and the Fort,* by Hervey Allen. Farrar & Rinehart

10. *The Song of Bernadette,* by Franz Werfel. Viking Press

NONFICTION

1. *Under Cover,* by John Roy Carlson. Dutton

2. *One World,* by Wendell L. Willkie. Simon & Schuster

3. *Journey Among Warriors,* by Eve Curie. Doubleday, Doran

4. *On Being a Real Person,* by Harry Emerson Fosdick. Harper

5. *Guadalcanal Diary,* by Richard Tregaskis. Random House

6. *Burma Surgeon,* by Lt. Col. Gordon Seagrave. Norton

7. *Our Hearts Were Young and Gay,* by Cornelia Otis Skinner and Emily Kimbrough. Dodd, Mead

8. *U. S. Foreign Policy,* by Walter Lippmann. Little, Brown

9. *Here Is Your War,* by Ernie Pyle. Holt

10. *See Here, Private Hargrove,* by Marion Hargrove. Holt

1944

FICTION

1. *Strange Fruit,* by Lillian Smith. Reynal & Hitchcock
2. *The Robe,* by Lloyd C. Douglas. Houghton Mifflin
3. *A Tree Grows in Brooklyn,* by Betty Smith. Harper
4. *Forever Amber,* by Kathleen Winsor. Macmillan
5. *The Razor's Edge,* by W. Somerset Maugham. Doubleday, Doran
6. *The Green Years,* by A. J. Cronin. Little, Brown
7. *Leave Her to Heaven,* by Ben Ames Williams. Houghton Mifflin
8. *Green Dolphin Street,* by Elizabeth Goudge. Coward-McCann
9. *A Bell for Adano,* by John Hersey. Knopf
10. *The Apostle,* by Sholem Asch. Putnam

NONFICTION

1. *I Never Left Home,* by Bob Hope. Simon & Schuster; Home Guide
2. *Brave Men,* by Ernie Pyle. Holt
3. *Good Night, Sweet Prince,* by Gene Fowler. Viking Press
4. *Under Cover,* by John Roy Carlson. Dutton
5. *Yankee from Olympus,* by Catherine Drinker Bowen. Little, Brown
6. *The Time for Decision,* by Sumner Welles. Harper
7. *Here Is Your War,* by Ernie Pyle. Holt
8. *Anna and the King of Siam,* by Margaret Landon. John Day
9. *The Curtain Rises,* by Quentin Reynolds. Random House
10. *Ten Years in Japan,* by Joseph C. Grew. Simon & Schuster

1945

FICTION

1. *Forever Amber,* by Kathleen Winsor. Macmillan

2. *The Robe,* by Lloyd C. Douglas. Houghton Mifflin

3. *The Black Rose,* by Thomas B. Costain. Doubleday

4. *The White Tower,* by James Ramsey Ullman. Lippincott

5. *Cass Timberlane,* by Sinclair Lewis. Random House

6. *A Lion Is in the Streets,* by Adria Locke Langley. Whittlesey House

7. *So Well Remembered,* by James Hilton. Little, Brown

8. *Captain from Castile,* by Samuel Shellabarger. Little, Brown

9. *Earth and High Heaven,* by Gwethalyn Graham. Lippincott

10. *Immortal Wife,* by Irving Stone. Doubleday

NONFICTION

1. *Brave Men,* by Ernie Pyle. Holt

2. *Dear Sir,* by Juliet Lowell. Duell, Sloan & Pearce

3. *Up Front,* by Bill Mauldin. Holt

4. *Black Boy,* by Richard Wright. Harper

5. *Try and Stop Me,* by Bennett Cerf. Simon & Schuster

6. *Anything Can Happen,* by George and Helen Papashvily. Harper

7. *General Marshall's Report.* Simon & Schuster

8. *The Egg and I,* by Betty MacDonald. Lippincott

9. *The Thurber Carnival,* by James Thurber. Harper

10. *Pleasant Valley,* by Louis Bromfield. Harper

1946

FICTION

1. *The King's General,* by Daphne du Maurier. Doubleday

2. *This Side of Innocence,* by Taylor Caldwell. Scribner

3. *The River Road,* by Frances Parkinson Keyes. Messner

4. *The Miracle of the Bells,* by Russell Janney. Prentice Hall

5. *The Hucksters,* by Frederic Wakeman. Rinehart

6. *The Foxes of Harrow,* by Frank Yerby. Dial Press

7. *Arch of Triumph,* by Erich Maria Remarque. Appleton-Century

8. *The Black Rose,* by Thomas B. Costain. Doubleday

9. *B. F.'s Daughter,* by John P. Marquand. Little, Brown

10. *The Snake Pit,* by Mary Jane Ward. Random House

NONFICTION

1. *The Egg and I,* by Betty MacDonald. Lippincott

2. *Peace of Mind,* by Joshua L. Liebman. Simon & Schuster

3. *As He Saw It,* by Elliott Roosevelt. Duell, Sloan & Pearce

4. *The Roosevelt I Knew,* by Frances Perkins. Viking Press

5. *Last Chapter,* by Ernie Pyle. Holt

6. *Starling of the White House,* by Thomas Sugrue and Col. Edmund Starling. Simon & Schuster

7. *I Chose Freedom,* by Victor Kravchenko. Scribner

8. *The Anatomy of Peace,* by Emery Reves. Harper

9. *Top Secret,* by Ralph Ingersoll. Harcourt, Brace

10. *A Solo in Tom-Toms,* by Gene Fowler. Viking Press

1947

FICTION

1. *The Miracle of the Bells,* by Russell Janney. Prentice-Hall

2. *The Moneyman,* by Thomas B. Costain. Doubleday

3. *Gentleman's Agreement,* by Laura Z. Hobson. Simon & Schuster

4. *Lydia Bailey,* by Kenneth Roberts. Doubleday

5. *The Vixens,* by Frank Yerby. Dial Press

6. *The Wayward Bus,* by John Steinbeck. Houghton Mifflin

7. *House Divided,* by Ben Ames Williams. Houghton Mifflin

8. *Kingsblood Royal,* by Sinclair Lewis. Random House

9. *East Side, West Side,* by Marcia Davenport. Scribner

10. *Prince of Foxes,* by Samuel Shellabarger. Little, Brown

NONFICTION

1. *Peace of Mind,* by Joshua L. Liebman. Simon & Schuster

2. *Information Please Almanac, 1947,* ed. by John Kieran. Garden City Publishing Co.

3. *Inside U. S. A.,* by John Gunther. Harper

4. *A Study of History,* by Arnold J. Toynbee. Oxford University Press

5. *Speaking Frankly,* by James F. Byrnes. Harper

6. *Human Destiny,* by Pierre Lecomte du Noüy. Longmans, Green

7. *The Egg and I,* by Betty MacDonald. Lippincott

8. *The American Past,* by Roger Butterfield. Simon & Schuster

9. *The Fireside Book of Folk Songs,* ed. by Margaret B. Boni. Simon & Schuster

10. *Together,* by Katharine T. Marshall. Tupper & Love

1948

FICTION

1. *The Big Fisherman,* by Lloyd C. Douglas. Houghton Mifflin

2. *The Naked and the Dead,* by Norman Mailer. Rinehart

3. *Dinner at Antoine's,* by Frances Parkinson Keyes. Messner

4. *The Bishop's Mantle,* by Agnes Sligh Turnbull. Macmillan

5. *Tomorrow Will Be Better,* by Betty Smith. Harper

6. *The Golden Hawk,* by Frank Yerby. Dial Press

7. *Raintree County,* by Ross Lockridge Jr. Houghton Mifflin

8. *Shannon's Way,* by A. J. Cronin. Little, Brown

9. *Pilgrim's Inn,* by Elizabeth Goudge. Coward-McCann

10. *The Young Lions,* by Irwin Shaw. Random House

NONFICTION

1. *Crusade in Europe,* by Dwight D. Eisenhower. Doubleday

2. *How to Stop Worrying and Start Living,* by Dale Carnegie. Simon & Schuster

3. *Peace of Mind,* by Joshua L. Liebman. Simon & Schuster

4. *Sexual Behavior in the Human Male,* by A. C. Kinsey and others. Saunders

5. *Wine, Women and Words,* by Billy Rose. Simon & Schuster

6. *The Life and Times of the Shmoo,* by Al Capp. Simon & Schuster

7. *The Gathering Storm,* by Winston Churchill. Houghton Mifflin

8. *Roosevelt and Hopkins,* by Robert E. Sherwood. Harper

9. *A Guide to Confident Living,* by Norman Vincent Peale. Prentice-Hall

10. *The Plague and I,* by Betty MacDonald. Lippincott

1949

FICTION

1. *The Egyptian,* by Mika Waltari. Putnam

2. *The Big Fisherman,* by Lloyd C. Douglas. Houghton Mifflin

3. *Mary,* by Sholem Asch. Putnam

4. *A Rage to Live,* by John O'Hara. Random House

5. *Point of No Return,* by John P. Marquand. Little, Brown

6. *Dinner at Antoine's,* by Frances Parkinson Keyes. Messner

7. *High Towers,* by Thomas B. Costain. Doubleday

8. *Cutlass Empire,* by Van Wyck Mason. Doubleday

9. *Pride's Castle,* by Frank Yerby. Dial Press

10. *Father of the Bride,* by Edward Streeter. Simon & Schuster

NONFICTION

1. *White Collar Zoo,* by Clare Barnes Jr. Doubleday

2. *How to Win at Canasta,* by Oswald Jacoby. Doubleday

3. *The Seven Storey Mountain,* by Thomas Merton. Harcourt, Brace

4. *Home Sweet Zoo,* by Clare Barnes Jr. Doubleday

5. *Cheaper by the Dozen,* by Frank B. Gilbreth Jr. and Ernestine Gilbreth Carey. Crowell

6. *The Greatest Story Ever Told,* by Fulton Oursler. Doubleday

7. *Canasta, the Argentine Rummy Game,* by Ottilie H. Reilly. Ives Washburn

8. *Canasta,* by Josephine Artayeta de Viel and Ralph Michael. Pellegrini & Cudahy

9. *Peace of Soul,* by Fulton J. Sheen. Whittlesey House

10. *A Guide to Confident Living,* by Norman Vincent Peale. Prentice-Hall

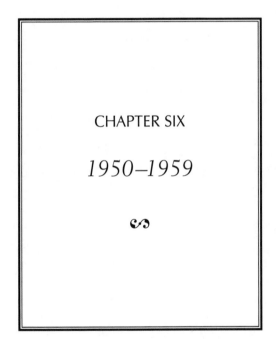

CHAPTER SIX

1950–1959

ભ

T HE NATURE OF THE FIFTIES as an era can be perfectly understood by a glance at the nonfiction bestseller list for 1950: *Betty Crocker's Picture Cook Book*; *The Baby*; *Look Younger, Live Longer*; *How I Raised Myself from Failure to Success in Selling*; *Your Dream Home*. The war had restored American productivity, brought a final end to the Great Depression, and made Americans yearn for a quiet life at home, in the new suburbs that were already redefining the American Way of Life. Succeeding at your job, buying your dream house, looking younger and living longer, and cooking food that looked pretty was what Americans wanted after the deprivations of the Depression and the excitement of war, though even as people settled into "the good life," the first tremors of change were taking place around them—in San Francisco "the Beats" were about to create the first wave of "counterculture," in the South the modern civil rights movement was starting, and in the colleges the staid conformity and soulless comfort of the early Eisenhower years were beginning to be criticized and ridiculed. People were reading Henry Morton Robinson's *The Cardinal*, the #1 bestselling novel of the year (which took on "The Powerhouse," as the Archdiocese of New York was then called). Book sales were soaring and the book clubs seemed like the wave of the future as everyone in the suburbs joined the Book-of-the-Month Club, the Literary Guild, or the *Reader's Digest* Condensed Book Club, but the worm was already in the apple of middle-class American life, which was being rejected even as millions of people sought to join it, and this would very shortly be reflected in the books on the bestseller list.

1951 was more of the same. Gayelord Hauser's *Look Younger, Live Longer* was still on the list—it didn't hurt that he was the diet and health guru and lover of Greta Garbo—and most of the nonfiction continued to represent an America involved in home, family, and looking good—*Betty Crocker's Picture Cook Book* (again), *Better Homes and Gardens Garden Book,* and *Better Homes and Gardens Handyman's Book.* The appearance on the list of *Pogo,* by Walt Kelly, signifies a rise of the new kind of comic strip to cult, as well as bestseller, status, soon to be followed by *Peanuts* and, eventually, *Doonesbury,* while the presence of Rachel Carson's *The Sea Around Us* is the first step toward environmentalism and the protection of nature—for many of us, including myself, an eye-opening book.

The Caine Mutiny and *From Here to Eternity* continued the trend of American popular fiction toward an antiwar (and anti–armed forces) stance, while Nicholas Monsarrat's *The Cruel Sea,* with its stiff-upper-lip officers and heroic sailors showed how widely Britain diverged from America in depicting the war. There is a deep gulf between the hard-bitten, courageous, and decent captain of Monsarrat's ship and Captain Queeg in Herman Wouk's, and henceforth there would be two very different views of the war in literature, the one emanating from America, and the other from the United Kingdom, both producing bestsellers.

In discussing the bestseller list, the *Bible* is always described as the ultimate bestseller, but in 1952, it actually hit the nonfiction list at #1, in the form of the Revised Standard Version, and sold over 2 million copies. The turn toward religion—those who remember the fifties will recall it as an age of piety, at least on the surface—is also exemplified by *A Man Called Peter,* an inspirational biography that sold in huge quantities, *The Power of Positive Thinking,* and *This I Believe.* Another major work of the 1950s was Whittaker Chambers's *Witness,* in which the man who had testified that Alger Hiss was a Communist wrote at length of his own life in the Party and the path that led him to becoming an informer.

On the fiction front, the most notable and long-lasting book was Ernest Hemingway's *The Old Man and the Sea,* which, partly because of its brevity and its lesson of stoic courage and endurance, is on school reading lists today. I remember reading it twice—as soon as I finished, I started to read it again—though that may partly be ascribed to the fact that I was in recruit training, beginning my national service in the Royal Air Force, when I did so. In any event, it bowled me over so hard that I have been unwilling to go back and read it again since then, on the grounds that I would either be disappointed in the book or in my own judgment.

In 1953 *seven* of the ten books on the nonfiction bestseller list were religious or inspirational, which so far as I know stands as a record. The fiction was nothing to write home about, though it included *Désirée,* a French bodice ripper that raised the bar in sexy fiction from where it had been after the publication of *Forever Amber.*

Anybody who wants to gauge for themselves the total vacuity of life and letters in the mid-1950s should look at the bestseller list for 1954. Half the novels on the list were historicals, none of which is remembered today, with the possible exception of Mika Waltari's *The Egyptian* (a reissue), and most of the nonfiction list was again dominated by religious books and cookbooks, the one big exception being singer Lillian Roth's *I'll Cry Tomorrow,* maybe the first of the really big tearjerker, scandalous biographies of show business figures, which would open up a whole new genre that was still producing bestsellers almost fifty years later.

In 1955, however, the dam broke, and a certain number of big new books brought some new energy and talent to the list, indicating, perhaps, that the end of the Eisenhower years was drawing nigh. Herman Wouk's *Marjorie Morningstar,* love it or leave it, at #1, was a book that broke new ground in making a famously Jewish heroine the center of a big, serious, romantic novel for the first time; Sloan Wilson's *The Man in the Gray Flannel Suit* exposed the hypocrisy of business and advertising; while Françoise Sagan's *Bonjour Tristesse* jumped the language and culture barrier that usually separates French fiction from American readers, and gained her a huge American following, which, unfortunately, she was unable, or perhaps, being French, unwilling to please in the future.

Since the list also included MacKinlay Kantor's *Andersonville*, a book I can remember to this day, Robert Ruark's *Something of Value*, which I couldn't put down and would probably work for me even today, and Patrick Dennis's sophisticated spoof *Auntie Mame*, fiction readers had nothing to complain about. Nonfiction books not only got the first book to hit the list from Billy Graham—a one-man publishing industry—but, more telling, *Why Johnny Can't Read*, the first book really to question the values and the results of the comfortable suburban life and to suggest behind the glossy, calm surface that whole areas—in this case, the schools—were hardly functioning at all. 1956 would continue the blandness of the nonfiction list—the #1 bestseller of the year was *Arthritis and Common Sense*, together with two cookbooks, a home decorating guide, an etiquette book, and three inspirational or religious books, but the fiction list reveals two major works, one *Peyton Place*, by Grace Metalious, one of the bestselling novels of all time—and in its own way a classic of weepy, tell-all sexy fiction, auguring in a new age in which Boston no longer banned books, and the big bestselling authors would be Harold Robbins, Jacqueline Susann, and Jackie Collins—and the other Simone de Beauvoir's *The Mandarins*, an uncompromisingly highbrow look at French political and literary life, the success of which cannot have been based on the fact that the author was the companion of Jean-Paul Sartre.

Nothing better illustrates the curiously bipolar nature of the American reader than the appearance on the list of Grace Metalious and Simone de
Beauvoir at the same time. One could argue that they were probably read by
different people, but I'm not even sure of that, frankly. The answer may be
that Americans craved culture—and the feeling that they were cultured
themselves—almost as much as they did a big tearjerker with a lot of sex.

Something of the same can be gleaned from the bestseller list of 1957.
The nonfiction list is mostly merchandise and books that have been created
only for their commercial possibilities: Art Linkletter's *Kids Say the Darndest
Things!* (soon to spawn a whole new industry of TV and book-related merchandise), Norman Vincent Peale's *Stay Alive All Your Life*; *Better Homes and
Gardens Flower Arranging Book*; Jim Bishop's lachrymose *The Day Christ
Died*, perhaps the first of the books in which popular journalists used their
skills to write history as if they were reporting it; *The American Heritage Book
of Great Historic Places*—the first of an avalanche of full-color merchandise
presented as history, in the guise of what would soon be called "coffee table"
books, implying (correctly) that they were purchased to be seen, not to be
read—but it also contains Jean Kerr's *Please Don't Eat the Daisies,* a book that
remains, at least in my memory, refreshingly alive and funny.

1958 is memorable to me because in August of that year I started work at
Simon & Schuster. Although the nonfiction list remained the kind of thumping,
predictable bore it had been through most of the fifties, the fiction list showed
that thirst for quality, or at least the illusion of serious importance, that was to
characterize a portion of the fiction list henceforth. Boris Pasternak's *Doctor
Zhivago* was #1, while Vladimir Nabokov's *Lolita* was at #3. The huge numbers
of the past were no longer happening in hardcover—*Lolita* sold about 150,000
copies, *Doctor Zhivago* about half a million (not counting book club sales).

These are respectable numbers, but most of the people who reach the top of the fiction list today expect to sell over a million copies or more. The big numbers in 1958 were in mass-market sales, which dwarfed those of hardcover books—indeed, back in those days, it looked as if the tail were now definitely starting to wag the dog, and when I joined S&S everybody told me that I was going to work for the wrong side of the business, that mass-market paperbacks were the wave of the future and that the hardcover book would soon be extinct, except for the kind of effete people who read arty first novels and collected books. Even hardcover book publishers took a dismal view of their future, which is why so many of them would sell out over the next few years, beginning that chain of mergers and acquisitions that have reduced the number of major publishing corporations to four or five. In the meantime, the mass-market business thrived, crested, then declined sharply, as the price of their books soared and they were exposed to the fierce competition of new technologies for the entertainment dollar, while hardcover sales, instead of vanishing, rose to mass-market levels, partly because of heavy discounting, which eventually made the hardcover book hardly more expensive than the mass-market book, and partly because in an increasingly prosperous and impatient world, nobody wanted to wait a year for the paperback edition of a hardcover book to appear. None of this, mind you, could have been foreseen in 1958, as I sat down behind a desk at S&S to start reading "the slush pile" of unsolicited manuscripts.

What I did realize, right away, is the huge role the bestseller played in our lives. In those days, the *New York Times* made something of a secret of the list, but for publishers, naturally, it was important to know the good news (or bad) as far ahead as possible, so they could tell the happy author, and, in those simpler days, inform the bookstores, if necessary, to order another printing of the book, and prepare "best seller ads" in advance. The order of books on the list was decided upon at the *Times* on Wednesday for the list that would appear in the *New York Times Book Review* on Sunday of the following week, and the publicity departments of the major publishing companies competed to cultivate "a friend at the *Times*" who would give them the list by telephone by Wednesday in the late afternoon. People stayed late on Wednesdays at S&S, waiting for the call from the publicity department. If it was good news, they ran shouting down the hall, from office to office, while Bob Gottlieb and Nina Bourne started to write ads, and Dick Grossman called "the accounts" and the sales reps to alert the bookstores. Even the normally reclusive Max Schuster, cofounder with Richard Simon of S&S, stayed late on Wednesdays to hear what the list was, and to call an especially important S&S author when he or she "hit the list"—Will Durant, say. It was, in short, a big deal.

Stories about how the list was drawn up abounded—how certain bookstores reported to the list because of some long-forgotten favor or attraction, how the list favored stores in the Midwest to counterbalance any Boston/New York City/Washington bias, how the people who compiled the list did a little mental juggling to favor the kind of books they thought ought to be on the list, as opposed to those they thought shouldn't be (like *Peyton Place,* for example), or to avoid a nonfiction list that consisted entirely of diet and self-help books.

Whether these stories were true or not, who knows, but in 1958 I used to sit around in the office in the evening on Wednesdays, sipping Jack Daniel's out of a paper cup in the company of my peers, five or six of us crammed into the office of Bob Gottlieb, the legendary S&S editor, waiting for the call, and listening to stories about the list—how so-and-so's wife had waited to divorce him until his book fell off the list, how so-and-so had gone out and bought an expensive new car on hearing that his book had made the list, only to learn that his editor had been mistaken, and mixed his book up with somebody else's, how the lady at the *Times* who prepared the final list had refused huge offers from movie company story editors to slip them the news before the publishers and agents heard it. . . . Then the phone would ring, and Bob would pick it up, grab a piece of paper, and with a frown of concentration and a Napoleonic lock of hair falling over his brow, write down the titles and the numbers.

As it happened, 1958 was a bad year for S&S, made worse by the fact that Jerome Weidman's novel *The Enemy Camp*, about relationships between Jews and Gentiles—a book Bob particularly disliked—hit the list and stayed there for some time, doubly wounding because Weidman had not only been an S&S author, but an S&S editor, and left for Random House after some unpleasantness and disagreement. 1959 wasn't much better, since the only book from S&S to hit the year's list was Alexander King's *Mine Enemy Grows Older*, an autobiography of an artist and television talk show regular that was edited by Peter Schwed, Bob Gottlieb's rival, and a book that all the younger people at S&S disliked, perhaps as a result. That apart, the 1959 list contained some interesting landmarks. First of all, *Lady Chatterley's Lover*, by D. H. Lawrence, hit the list at #5, after a fiercely fought legal struggle ended, once and for all, any censorship over books. Formerly, *Lady Chatterley's Lover* was one of those books—like Henry Miller's—that you could only get in Paris, and had to bring back into the United States (and the United Kingdom) secreted in your baggage, at the risk of having it confiscated by a customs officer. Now, it was on sale at bookstores all over the United States, in a signal victory for Grove Press, and for S&S director Ephraim London, who fought the case all the way to the United States Supreme Court, sitting on the same shelves as Pat Boone's *Twixt Twelve and Twenty* (at #1 on the nonfiction list).

Not every bookstore was happy about this victory, by the way. Booksellers had hitherto been spared the quandary of whether to carry "dirty" books (and thereby offend many of their customers) because books like *Lady Chatterley's Lover* simply weren't available legally. Now that they at last had the right to sell them, they had to decide whether to display them or not, and many did not. All the same, the Grove Press victory would very shortly have a huge effect on bookselling, both in terms of literary freedom, and in terms of books like Dr. Alex Comfort's *The Joy of Sex,* the illustrations of which would have landed a bookseller in jail before 1959, but were soon to become commonplace in bookstores across America. It was also a larger, societal change, a kind of shifting of the tectonic plates in the American consciousness. Not all that many people were thrilled by reading *Lady Chatterley's Lover* when push came to shove and they could go to the bookstore and buy it, but the decision revealed, like nothing else, that beneath the placid surface of the late 1950s, American attitudes toward sex—and many other things—had changed radically. We had not yet reached the era of sex, drugs, and rock and roll, but it was, so to speak, just around the corner, and if you didn't believe it, all you had to do was go to your local bookstore and see for yourself that they were selling, among the Bibles and the cookbooks, the book that for decades people had brought home from Paris hidden in their dirty underwear, and passed around from hand to hand until it fell to pieces.

The rest of the 1959 list pales by comparison, although it is worth noting that Harry Golden had two books of nostalgia about Jewish life on the list at the same time, while Leon Uris's *Exodus* was #1. Being Jewish was now mainstream, only twelve years after Laura Z. Hobson's *Gentleman's Agreement* reached the list, making it seem old-fashioned, and the number of Jewish bestselling fiction writers was increasing dramatically, even as a new generation of Jewish writers, some of them more literary like Philip Roth, others who were inventing a new form of "dark humor," including

Joseph Heller, Bruce Jay Friedman, and Wallace Markfield, began to emerge. In the meantime, much of the list was business as usual—*Folk Medicine,* by a Vermont doctor, *The General Foods Kitchen Cookbook,* etc.—except for the appearance of Moss Hart's luminous *Act One,* perhaps the best show biz memoir ever written and still a great "read" today.

One thing the decade made clear: The fiction list would increasingly consist of big "blockbuster" novels, with a big subject and a big story, by "name" authors, books that could be read by men as well as women, like James Michener's *Hawaii* or Leon Uris's *Exodus,* followed by "women's" novels, whether romantic or sexy. The fiction bestseller lists of earlier decades that were dominated by historical romances had given way to what might be described as a basically "unisex" list. To take 1959 as an example, *Doctor Zhivago, Advise and Consent, Exodus, Hawaii, The Ugly American, Lolita,* and *Poor No More* were novels that were probably as much read by men as by women, leaving only *Dear and Glorious Physician* and *Mrs. 'Arris Goes to Paris* as "women's fiction," with *Lady Chatterley's Lover* a question mark, more of a curiosity than anything else.

Henceforth there would be at one extreme "romantic" novels, at the other the big "techno thrillers" (still to come), but most of the novels on the list would fall in between the extremes, and appealed to men and women alike. This argues for three other conclusions about the end of the fifties— first, that men were reading more fiction; second, that fewer writers sat down to write specifically for men or for women; and finally, that fewer women readers of fiction confined themselves to romantic or romantic historical novels.

Women had, in effect, joined the mainstream, in terms of education and of their interests, and this, like so much else in American society, was being reflected in the bestseller list.

1950

FICTION

1. *The Cardinal,* by Henry Morton Robinson. Simon & Schuster

2. *Joy Street,* by Frances Parkinson Keyes. Messner

3. *Across the River and Into the Trees,* by Ernest Hemingway. Scribner

4. *The Wall,* by John Hersey. Knopf

5. *Star Money,* by Kathleen Winsor. Appleton-Century-Crofts

6. *The Parasites,* by Daphne du Maurier. Doubleday

7. *Floodtide,* by Frank Yerby. Dial Press

8. *Jubilee Trail,* by Gwen Bristow. Crowell

9. *The Adventurer,* by Mika Waltari. Putnam

10. *The Disenchanted,* by Budd Schulberg. Random House

NONFICTION

1. *Betty Crocker's Picture Cook Book.* McGraw-Hill

2. *The Baby.* Simon & Schuster

3. *Look Younger, Live Longer,* by Gayelord Hauser. Farrar, Straus & Young

4. *How I Raised Myself from Failure to Success in Selling,* by Frank Bettger. Prentice-Hall

5. *Kon-Tiki,* by Thor Heyerdahl. Rand McNally

6. *Mr. Jones, Meet the Master,* by Peter Marshall. Revell

7. *Your Dream Home,* by Hubbard Cobb. Wise

8. *The Mature Mind,* by H. A. Overstreet. Norton

9. *Campus Zoo,* by Clare Barnes Jr. Doubleday

10. *Belles on Their Toes,* by Frank Gilbreth Jr. and Ernestine Gilbreth Carey. Crowell

1951

FICTION

1. *From Here to Eternity,* by James Jones. Scribner

2. *The Caine Mutiny,* by Herman Wouk. Doubleday

3. *Moses,* by Sholem Asch. Putnam

4. *The Cardinal,* by Henry Morton Robinson. Simon & Schuster

5. *A Woman Called Fancy,* by Frank Yerby. Dial Press

6. *The Cruel Sea,* by Nicholas Monsarrat. Knopf

7. *Melville Goodwin, U. S. A.,* by John P. Marquand. Little, Brown

8. *Return to Paradise,* by James A. Michener. Random House

9. *The Foundling,* by Cardinal Spellman. Scribner

10. *The Wanderer,* by Mika Waltari. Putnam

NONFICTION

1. *Look Younger, Live Longer,* by Gayelord Hauser. Farrar, Straus & Young

2. *Betty Crocker's Picture Cook Book.* McGraw-Hill

3. *Washington Confidential,* by Jack Lait and Lee Mortimer. Crown

4. *Better Homes and Gardens Garden Book.* Meredith

5. *Better Homes and Gardens Handyman's Book.* Meredith

6. *The Sea Around Us,* by Rachel L. Carson. Oxford University Press

7. *Thorndike-Barnhart Comprehensive Desk Dictionary,* ed. by Clarence L. Barnhart. Doubleday

8. *Pogo,* by Walt Kelly. Simon & Schuster

9. *Kon-Tiki,* by Thor Heyerdahl. Rand McNally

10. *The New Yorker Twenty-Fifth Anniversary Album.* Harper

1952

FICTION

1. *The Silver Chalice,* by Thomas B. Costain. Doubleday

2. *The Caine Mutiny,* by Herman Wouk. Doubleday

3. *East of Eden,* by John Steinbeck. Viking Press

4. *My Cousin Rachel,* by Daphne du Maurier. Doubleday

5. *Steamboat Gothic,* by Frances Parkinson Keyes. Messner

6. *Giant,* by Edna Ferber. Doubleday

7. *The Old Man and the Sea,* by Ernest Hemingway. Scribner

8. *The Gown of Glory,* by Agnes Sligh Turnbull. Houghton Mifflin

9. *The Saracen Blade,* by Frank Yerby. Dial Press

10. *The Houses in Between,* by Howard Spring. Harper

NONFICTION

1. *The Holy Bible: Revised Standard Version.* Nelson

2. *A Man Called Peter,* by Catherine Marshall. McGraw-Hill

3. *U. S. A. Confidential,* by Jack Lait and Lee Mortimer. Crown

4. *The Sea Around Us,* by Rachel L. Carson. Oxford University Press

5. *Tallulah,* by Tallulah Bankhead. Harper

6. *The Power of Positive Thinking,* by Norman Vincent Peale. Prentice-Hall

7. *This I Believe,* ed. by Edward P. Morgan; foreword by Edward R. Murrow. Simon & Schuster

8. *This Is Ike,* ed. by Wilson Hicks. Holt

9. *Witness,* by Whittaker Chambers. Random House

10. *Mr. President,* by William Hillman. Farrar, Straus & Young

1953

FICTION

1. *The Robe,* by Lloyd C. Douglas. Houghton Mifflin

2. *The Silver Chalice,* by Thomas B. Costain. Doubleday

3. *Désirée,* by Annemarie Selinko. Morrow

4. *Battle Cry,* by Leon M. Uris. Putnam

5. *From Here to Eternity,* by James Jones. Scribner

6. *The High and the Mighty,* by Ernest K. Gann. Sloane

7. *Beyond This Place,* by A. J. Cronin. Little, Brown

8. *Time and Time Again,* by James Hilton. Little, Brown

9. *Lord Vanity,* by Samuel Shellabarger. Little, Brown

10. *The Unconquered,* by Ben Ames Williams. Houghton Mifflin

NONFICTION

1. *The Holy Bible: Revised Standard Version.* Nelson

2. *The Power of Positive Thinking,* by Norman Vincent Peale. Prentice-Hall

3. *Sexual Behavior in the Human Female,* by Alfred C. Kinsey and others. Saunders

4. *Angel Unaware,* by Dale Evans Rogers. Revell

5. *Life Is Worth Living,* by Fulton J. Sheen. McGraw-Hill

6. *A Man Called Peter,* by Catherine Marshall. McGraw-Hill

7. *This I Believe,* ed. by Edward P. Morgan; foreword by Edward R. Murrow. Simon & Schuster

8. *The Greatest Faith Ever Known,* by Fulton Oursler and G. A. O. Armstrong. Doubleday

9. *How to Play Your Best Golf,* by Tommy Armour. Simon & Schuster

10. *A House Is Not a Home,* by Polly Adler. Rinehart

1954

FICTION

1. *Not As a Stranger,* by Morton Thompson. Scribner

2. *Mary Anne,* by Daphne du Maurier. Doubleday

3. *Love Is Eternal,* by Irving Stone. Doubleday

4. *The Royal Box,* by Frances Parkinson Keyes. Messner

5. *The Egyptian,* by Mika Waltari. Putnam

6. *No Time for Sergeants,* by Mac Hyman. Random House

7. *Sweet Thursday,* by John Steinbeck. Viking Press

8. *The View from Pompey's Head,* by Hamilton Basso. Doubleday

9. *Never Victorious, Never Defeated,* by Taylor Caldwell. McGraw-Hill

10. *Benton's Row,* by Frank Yerby. Dial Press

NONFICTION

1. *The Holy Bible: Revised Standard Version.* Nelson

2. *The Power of Positive Thinking,* by Norman Vincent Peale. Prentice-Hall

3. *Better Homes and Gardens New Cook Book.* Meredith

4. *Betty Crocker's Good and Easy Cook Book.* Simon & Schuster

5. *The Tumult and the Shouting,* by Grantland Rice. A. S. Barnes

6. *I'll Cry Tomorrow,* by Lillian Roth, Gerold Frank and Mike Connolly.
   Frederick Fell

7. *The Prayers of Peter Marshall,* ed. by Catherine Marshall. McGraw-Hill

8. *This I Believe, 2,* ed. by Raymond Swing. Simon & Schuster

9. *But We Were Born Free,* by Elmer Davis. Bobbs-Merrill

10. *The Saturday Evening Post Treasury,* ed. by Roger Butterfield.
    Simon & Schuster

1955

FICTION

1. *Marjorie Morningstar,* by Herman Wouk. Doubleday

2. *Auntie Mame,* by Patrick Dennis. Vanguard Press

3. *Andersonville,* by MacKinlay Kantor. World Publishing Co.

4. *Bonjour Tristesse,* by Françoise Sagan. Dutton

5. *The Man in the Gray Flannel Suit,* by Sloan Wilson. Simon & Schuster

6. *Something of Value,* by Robert Ruark. Doubleday

7. *Not As a Stranger,* by Morton Thompson. Scribner

8. *No Time for Sergeants,* by Mac Hyman. Random House

9. *The Tontine,* by Thomas B. Costain. Doubleday

10. *Ten North Frederick,* by John O'Hara. Random House

NONFICTION

1. *Gifts from the Sea,* by Anne Morrow Lindbergh. Pantheon Books

2. *The Power of Positive Thinking,* by Norman Vincent Peale. Prentice-Hall

3. *The Family of Man,* by Edward Steichen. Simon & Schuster and Maco Magazine Corp.

4. *A Man Called Peter,* by Catherine Marshall. McGraw-Hill

5. *How to Live 365 Days a Year,* by John A. Schindler. Prentice-Hall

6. *Better Homes and Gardens Diet Book.* Meredith

7. *The Secret of Happiness,* by Billy Graham. Doubleday

8. *Why Johnny Can't Read,* by Rudolf Flesch. Harper

9. *Inside Africa,* by John Gunther. Harper

10. *Year of Decisions,* by Harry S. Truman. Doubleday

1956

FICTION

1. *Don't Go Near the Water,* by William Brinkley. Random House

2. *The Last Hurrah,* by Edwin O'Connor. Little, Brown

3. *Peyton Place,* by Grace Metalious. Messner

4. *Auntie Mame,* by Patrick Dennis. Vanguard Press

5. *Eloise,* by Kay Thompson. Simon & Schuster

6. *Andersonville,* by MacKinlay Kantor. World Publishing Co.

7. *A Certain Smile,* by Françoise Sagan. Dutton

8. *The Tribe That Lost Its Head,* by Nicholas Monsarrat. Sloane

9. *The Mandarins,* by Simone de Beauvoir. World Publishing Co.

10. *Boon Island,* by Kenneth Roberts. Doubleday

NONFICTION

1. *Arthritis and Common Sense. Revised Edition,* by Dan Dale Alexander. Witkower Press

2. *Webster's New World Dictionary of the American Language. Concise Edition,* ed. by David B. Guralnik. World Publishing Co.

3. *Betty Crocker's Picture Cook Book. Revised and Enlarged Second Edition.* McGraw-Hill

4. *Etiquette,* by Frances Benton. Random House

5. *Better Homes and Gardens Barbecue Book.* Meredith

6. *The Search for Bridey Murphy,* by Morey Bernstein. Doubleday

7. *Love or Perish,* by Smiley Blanton, M. D. Simon & Schuster

8. *Better Homes and Gardens Decorating Book.* Meredith

9. *How to Live 365 Days a Year,* by John A. Schindler. Prentice-Hall

10. *The Nun's Story,* by Kathryn Hulme. Little, Brown

1957

FICTION

1. *By Love Possessed,* by James Gould Cozzens. Harcourt, Brace

2. *Peyton Place,* by Grace Metalious. Messner

3. *Compulsion,* by Meyer Levin. Simon & Schuster

4. *Rally Round the Flag, Boys!* by Max Shulman. Doubleday

5. *Blue Camellia,* by Frances Parkinson Keyes. Messner

6. *Eloise in Paris,* by Kay Thompson. Simon & Schuster

7. *The Scapegoat,* by Daphne du Maurier. Doubleday

8. *On the Beach,* by Nevil Shute. Morrow

9. *Below the Salt,* by Thomas B. Costain. Doubleday

10. *Atlas Shrugged,* by Ayn Rand. Random House

NONFICTION

1. *Kids Say the Darndest Things!* by Art Linkletter. Prentice-Hall

2. *The FBI Story,* by Don Whitehead. Random House

3. *Stay Alive All Your Life,* by Norman Vincent Peale. Prentice-Hall

4. *To Live Again,* by Catherine Marshall. McGraw-Hill

5. *Better Homes and Gardens Flower Arranging.* Meredith

6. *Where Did You Go? Out. What Did You Do? Nothing,* by Robert Paul Smith. Norton

7. *Baruch: My Own Story,* by Bernard M. Baruch. Holt

8. *Please Don't Eat the Daisies,* by Jean Kerr. Doubleday

9. *The American Heritage Book of Great Historic Places.* American Heritage Publishing Co. and Simon & Schuster

10. *The Day Christ Died,* by Jim Bishop. Harper

1958

FICTION

1. *Doctor Zhivago,* by Boris Pasternak. Pantheon Books

2. *Anatomy of a Murder,* by Robert Traver. St. Martin's

3. *Lolita,* by Vladimir Nabokov. Putnam

4. *Around the World with Auntie Mame,* by Patrick Dennis. Harcourt, Brace

5. *From the Terrace,* by John O'Hara. Random House

6. *Eloise at Christmastime,* by Kay Thompson. Random House

7. *Ice Palace,* by Edna Ferber. Doubleday

8. *The Winthrop Woman,* by Anya Seton. Houghton, Mifflin

9. *The Enemy Camp,* by Jerome Weidman. Random House

10. *Victorine,* by Frances Parkinson Keyes. Messner

NONFICTION

1. *Kids Say the Darndest Things!* by Art Linkletter. Prentice-Hall

2. *'Twixt Twelve and Twenty,* by Pat Boone. Prentice-Hall

3. *Only in America,* by Harry Golden. World Publishing Co.

4. *Masters of Deceit,* by Edgar Hoover. Holt

5. *Please Don't Eat the Daisies,* by Jean Kerr. Doubleday

6. *Better Homes and Gardens Salad Book.* Meredith Publishing Co.

7. *The New Testament in Modern English,* translated by J. P. Phillips. Macmillan

8. *Aku-Aku,* by Thor Heyerdahl. Rand McNally

9. *Dear Abby,* by Abigal Van Buren. Prentice-Hall

10. *Inside Russia Today,* by John Gunther. Harper

1959

FICTION

1. *Exodus,* by Leon Uris. Doubleday

2. *Doctor Zhivago,* by Boris Pasternak. Pantheon Books

3. *Hawaii,* by James Michener. Random House

4. *Advise and Consent,* by Allen Drury. Doubleday

5. *Lady Chatterley's Lover,* by D. H. Lawrence. Grove Press

6. *The Ugly American,* by William J. Lederer and Eugene L. Burdick. Norton

7. *Dear and Glorious Physician,* by Taylor Caldwell. Doubleday

8. *Lolita,* by Vladimir Nabokov. Putnam

9. *Mrs. 'Arris Goes to Paris,* by Paul Gallico. Doubleday

10. *Poor No More,* by Robert Ruark. Holt

NONFICTION

1. *'Twixt Twelve and Twenty,* by Pat Boone. Prentice-Hall

2. *Folk Medicine,* by D. C. Jarvis. Holt

3. *For 2¢ Plain,* by Harry Golden. World Publishing Co.

4. *The Status Seekers,* by Vance Packard. McKay

5. *Act One,* by Moss Hart. Random House

6. *Charley Weaver's Letters from Mamma,* by Cliff Arquette. Winston

7. *Elements of Style,* by William Strunk Jr. and E. B. White. Macmillan

8. *The General Foods Kitchens Cookbook.* Random House

9. *Only in America,* by Harry Golden. World Publishing Co.

10. *Mine Enemy Grows Older,* by Alexander King. Simon & Schuster

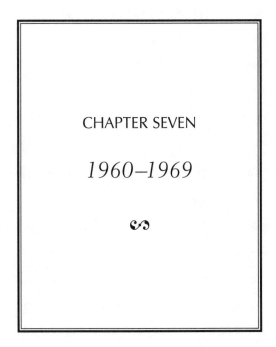

CHAPTER SEVEN

1960–1969

&

T HE 1 9 6 0 s ! In 1960 I edited Irving Wallace's *The Chapman Report*, which went to #4 on the year's list and made him a rich man, and earned me a raise of something like twenty-five dollars a week. I remember that Wallace went out and bought a Bentley. I can't remember what I bought—a good bottle of wine, I hope.

The 1960 nonfiction list contained another volume of Alexander King's memoirs, to the consternation of those at his publisher who hadn't liked the first volume, and also a book that remains in print and widely read over forty years later, William L. Shirer's *The Rise and Fall of the Third Reich*. Perhaps most notably, Barry Goldwater's *Conscience of a Conservative* appeared at #8, a sign that even as John F. Kennedy prepared for his first year in office, the conservative movement was already beginning to attract followers in large numbers, for whom a whole host of issues, ranging from Jack and Jackie themselves to "smutty" novels, "radical" books, evolution, fluoridation, and "humanism" were anathema.

Publishers, by and large, lived in New York City (except for the few who lived then in Boston and Philadelphia) and most of them were "progressive" in a mild way, "liberal" in the sense that New York City itself was liberal. Book readers, the review media, the publishing industry as a whole, were, seen from west of the Hudson, people who believed in certain liberal values. Unlike television and the movie industry, book publishing was not sufficiently important or glamorous, as seen from Washington, to attract the attention of Senator Joseph McCarthy or the House Un-American Activities Committee, so most publishers and editors had by and large been spared "the black list" and the witch-hunts of the late forties and the early fifties. Still, I remember going to a book publication party in Alger Hiss's apartment early in my publishing career, which is not something most people in the movie business would have done at the time, and several of the editors and many of the authors were victims of the Red Hunt.

That is not to say that book publishers were leftists, but they were, as sophisticated, urban people, many of them Jewish, inclined to vote Democratic rather than Republican; certainly very few of them were, to use a phrase of the thirties and early forties, "Roosevelt hissers" (referring to those who hissed FDR at the movies whenever he appeared in the newsreels). "Instant" books (a new category for books on current events that were rushed out in a hurry) had proliferated around President and Mrs. Kennedy from the very beginning; the defeat of Nixon had come as a relief to lots of people in the book publishing world (I speak as one who later became Nixon's editor and a friend). With a Democrat back in the White House, and, moreover, a Harvard-educated Democrat, who wrote and read books and surrounded himself with "progressive" figures from academia, many in publishing were feeling that "all's right with the world," to quote a Robert Browning poem.

Given this, the success of Barry Goldwater's *Conscience of a Conservative* took book publishers by surprise, and made not a few of them nervous. Others did a fast calculation in their head, and figured it might not be a bad idea to publish both ends of the spectrum. In that sense, Goldwater's book was a breakthrough for the many big conservative bestsellers to come, an indication that there was a lot of money to be made on the right, whether you agreed with them or not. The bookselling community was by and large liberal, too, even in the Deep South, so they, too, were at first unwilling to believe that conservative books would sell in large numbers until Barry Goldwater came along. Book publishers had always been less liberal than their editors, and much less liberal than their authors, but much of the old received wisdom about politics and publishing was about to change, as "the conservative movement," a blanket phrase covering a lot of different political phenomena, began to grow, and was no longer seen as one of those West Coast fads—"little old ladies in tennis shoes."

1961 was a landmark year of sorts for fiction. The publication of Henry Miller's *Tropic of Cancer* by Grove Press—another of those books that people used to have to smuggle in from Paris—drove the final nail in the coffin of censorship, so far as books were concerned, while the publication of *The Carpetbaggers,* Harold Robbins's sex-laden riff on the life of Howard Hughes, broke new ground for popular fiction. Irving Stone's *The Agony and the Ecstasy* (Michelangelo vs. the Pope) and Leon Uris's *Mila 18* (the Warsaw Ghetto uprising against the Germans) were typical of the big, muscular new kind of bestseller, while J. D. Salinger rose to #2 with *Franny and Zooey,* to prove that literature could still win large numbers of readers. But wait, look at this list: Irving Stone, J. D. Salinger, Harper Lee's *To Kill a Mockingbird,* Leon Uris, Henry Miller, Morris West, Edwin O'Connor's *The Edge of Sadness,* John Steinbeck—no mysteries, no romances, no bodice rippers, not a single conventional "women's novel"—this is a list of big, ambitious novels, written at different levels, certainly, from downright clunky to literary, but suggesting that American readers of both genders had come of age at last. True, the nonfiction list includes a sewing book, a casserole cookbook, a nutrition book, and Dr. Herman Taller's *Calories Don't Count,* one of the most successful diet books ever published (though it shortly turned out to be a page-one scandal when it became apparent that calories *did* count, after all). In short, American book buyers in 1961 still had the same nonfiction interests as their parents.

In the publishing world, paperback sales were still rising, the general feeling being that the mass-market business would eventually take over the hardcover business, reducing hardcover books to a kind of boutique status.

As a result of this, the prices that paperback publishers were paying for the rights to successful books escalated abruptly. Only a year or two earlier, $100,000 was a huge amount to pay for mass-market rights to a bestseller, but Fawcett paid an eyebrow-raising $400,000 for the paperback rights to *The Rise and Fall of the Third Reich,* and within the decade a million dollars and more would become commonplace.

What is more, paperback publishers were beginning to enter the hard-cover field. *The Carpetbaggers* was, in fact, published in hardcover by Pocket Books (though under a different name, Trident Press), and book publishers soon found that while their bottom line depended on mass-market advances, the mass-market publishers were, at the same time, becoming their competitors. One result of all this was that the mass-market books began to find their way into the bookstores, despite a certain initial reluctance on the part of booksellers. Another, even more far reaching, was the first, hesitant steps to sell hardcover books at a discount. Hitherto, the retail price set by the publisher was adhered to except during annual sales, when the store's overstock was marked down. Book publishers were as puzzled as everyone else by the new retailing phenomenon of discounting, which began with appliances. A block away from S&S was the warehouse-type store of Three Guys from Brooklyn, where, if you were willing to push and struggle to catch a salesman's attention in the general chaos, you could buy an air conditioner for half of what you'd pay in a department store or a regular appliance store. Of course you had to be able to lug it home in its box, which made these stores gravitate naturally toward the suburbs where you could drive your car right up to the loading dock, and you were on your own when it came to service and installation, but in the meantime you had saved a bundle. GE and all the big appliance manufacturers were at first as determined to protect their list price as the book publishers were, but once they realized that discounting increased sales, they gave in—and indeed, a series of court decisions would eventually confirm what the marketplace was already doing, by preventing manufacturers from setting arbitrary list prices, thus giving birth to the phrase "manufacturer's suggested list price," which was itself an unenforceable fiction. Thus, while S&S and all the major book publishers struggled to maintain the list prices of their books, the future was around the corner, in our case on West 48th Street, where the same people who thought the list price of a book was sacrosanct were queuing up at lunchtime to buy an air conditioner at one-third off list.

The big revolution in book publishing would not come from the publishers, whose last big change was to make books returnable during the Depression; it would come, instead, from the retailers, particularly the growing number of chain stores, whose customers were getting used to the idea of buying things at a discount, many of whom had never been in one of the old-fashioned bookstores where the atmosphere was hushed and literary in tone, the sense of display rudimentary, and in which you might hesitate before asking for a copy of *The Carpetbaggers* or *Tropic of Cancer*. Besides, these stores were usually open from ten o'clock in the morning to five in the evening, and closed on Sundays, of course. In fact, at just the times when the average person might want to buy a book—after work, or late in the evening, or Sunday shopping—the bookstores were closed.

Some of the chain stores, like the Doubleday stores in New York City, made a point of staying open late for night owls, but in general the retail book business operated on banker's hours, which helped to explain the popularity of mass-market books. Mass-market paperbacks were hard to read with their tiny print, and fell apart quickly, but they mostly sold in places that were open at night and on the weekends, like drugstores and newsstands. The impulse to change all this came from below, gradually, as the booksellers started to wake up to the dawn of a new kind of retailing that would come of age in the suburbs, and the publishers slowly came to grips that it didn't really matter what price you printed on the front flap of the book if somebody out there was willing to sell it cheaper.

The 1962 fiction list once again showed the decline of the traditional "women's novel" and the old-fashioned "historical." It was dominated by Katherine Anne Porter's *Ship of Fools,* Herman Wouk's *Youngblood Hawke,* Irving Wallace's *The Prize* ("Wake up, you fool, you've won the Nobel Prize!"), but introduced a new phenomenon in the form of the political bestseller written by a journalist or a team of journalists, in this case Eugene Burdick and Harvey Wheeler, who wrote *Fail-Safe,* and Fletcher Knebel and Charles W. Bailey II, who wrote *Seven Days in May.* Hitherto, novels, good and bad, had been generally written by a single person (known as the novelist), but so far as I know these are the first two successful examples of novels written by a team of non-novelists. If a couple of newsmen could get together and cook up a bestselling novel that would go on to sell millions of copies in paperback and be made into a hugely successful film, why couldn't anybody? Publishers and agents were soon coming up with big subjects for novels themselves, and writers with the time on their hands, or successful journalists, to "novelize" (a new and dreadful word) them, thus opening up the way for what was referred to in publishing circles as the "non-novel."

In nonfiction, Americans were still mostly interested in losing weight and cooking, but one book stands out—Helen Gurley Brown's *Sex and the Single Girl* was #9, and signaled a huge change in American mores. Not only did Helen Gurley Brown write about sex frankly and give her single girls some of the sexual bravado that was later to characterize "That Cosmo Woman" when Ms. Brown took over *Cosmopolitan* magazine, but she hyped her book right onto the bestseller list by tirelessly plugging it on talk shows. From now on, publishers would be looking for nonfiction authors who could promote their own books on "the tube," as it was called, and the publicity department began to play a role in deciding whether or not to take a book on.

Sex and the Single Girl marks the beginning of a whole new era of bookselling, though still in its embryonic stage: a hot subject, a promotable author, a more direct connection between book publisher and bookstores, and early discounting. Bestselling books had always moved quickly—often too quickly for the publisher to do anything about it—but now they tended to leap on the list even more quickly, particularly when reviews, features, an appearance on a major talk show, and advertising coincided (making them coincide became an art form, the best test of a publisher's marketing skill). As a result, publishers no longer had the luxury of waiting for the numbers to come in before they printed more copies—the new marketplace would be one in which to make a big seller it was necessary to start off with an ambitious first printing, and where the first question from the booksellers would be, "How many copies are you printing?" You couldn't expect to do it anymore by printing 25,000 or 30,000 copies and watching carefully to see when it was time to print another 10,000 or so. You had to bite the bullet and commit to a first printing of 100,000 or more, if you wanted a book to work, and take the unpleasant consequences if a lot of them came back unsold. What had been a staid business was in the process of turning into a casino game, as publishing took on a "boom or bust" mentality. What mattered was not careful, long-term nurturing of talent, but guessing right, and backing your guess with a big printing, a lot of ads, and a promotion tour.

M.D., represents, however, a whole new kind of self-help, first of all because the book is Freudian, a criticism of the way people behave falsely toward others and toward themselves by role-playing, rather than being inspirational and keyed to teaching the reader how to get along with other people, and secondly because Berne was good on television, which did much to boost the sales of his book to over 200,000 copies. 1966, however, was a different vintage, a sign that the times were changing in the middle of the sixties, for it was the year of *Valley of the Dolls,* by Jacqueline Susann, which sold over 300,000 copies in hardcover, making it the #1 novel of the year, and would eventually sell nearly 10 million copies in paperback. *Valley of the Dolls* (or *"Dolls"* as its author called the book) was unashamedly a "women's novel," a romantic tearjerker in the Fannie Hurst tradition, but with a lot of fairly explicit sex and the additional cachet of being something of a *roman à clef* about Hollywood movie stars as well. The formula was not exactly new, but the addition of tough sexuality and movie stars to what was, at heart, a shop girl romance, brought Jackie Susann instant fame and fortune. Like Helen Gurley Brown, Jackie knew how to promote the book, too. The blend of TV appearances, bookstore visits, eye-catching advertising, and column planting that had worked for *Sex and the Single Girl* was freshened up and used again, but this time—a big change—for a novel. Not surprisingly, it worked, and pretty soon the publicity departments of the major publishers were vetting fiction writers as well as nonfiction ones and trying to figure out a "pitch" that would get a novelist on the *Tonight Show.* That Truman Capote's *In Cold Blood* was published in the same year is a delicious irony. Literary as he was, Capote was also a brilliant self-promoter who understood publicity, with the result that he and Jackie clashed head-on on television, making headlines everywhere. It was Capote who said of her, with his trademark lisp, "She doesn't write, she types!" And, nastier still, that she looked like a truck driver in drag. The feud between the two of them brought thousands of people into the bookstores who had never visited one before.

1967 was another great vintage for fiction. The bestsellers included Elia Kazan's *The Arrangement,* William Styron's *The Confessions of Nat Turner,* Chaim Potok's *The Chosen,* and Ira Levin's *Rosemary's Baby.* One would like to be able to travel back in time and read them again for the first time.

1968 saw two books reach the bestseller list that represented two "firsts." Rod McKuen's *Listen to the Warm* and *Lonesome Cities* were the first collections of poetry to hit the bestseller list in decades, and were also the first wave of a new kind of sensibility, a kind of West Coast, counterculture spirituality that was at once sentimental and, when read in the right spirit, close to rock lyrics, or, at times, Hallmark greeting cards. While McKuen was hardly radical—in his own way he was a modern version of Edgar Guest— he represented the first step onto the bestseller list of books that came out of the sensibility of a new generation, the generation that had grown up to the Beatles' music, aspired to run away to San Francisco, and fueled the growing antiwar protests. For these kids, *Valley of the Dolls* was the kind of book their mothers read, and while McKuen was a crossover figure—he appealed to old ladies as much as he did to flower children—he is the first person from that generation's background and sensibility to hit the bestseller list, except for John Lennon himself, who was such a celebrity that no rules apply to him. At any rate, between the success of Lennon's in the bookstores and the sales of Rod McKuen's poetry, publishers now had to think about how to appeal to the younger generation—no easy task, when most publishers were looking at their own kids and trying to figure out what on earth they had done wrong as a parent.

McKuen made the list again in 1969 with two more books, as prolific as he was promotable, along with *Linda Goodman's Sun Signs,* another signal that the counterculture could produce big bestsellers, as well as sex, drugs, and rock and roll. In fiction, 1969 produced one of the great bestsellers, Mario Puzo's *The Godfather,* but #1 went to Philip Roth's *Portnoy's Complaint* (vehemently attacked as "a novel about masturbation"), prompting Jackie Susann to remark on television that while she didn't mind meeting Roth, she didn't want to shake his hand.

Jackie herself was back, this time at Simon & Schuster with me as her editor, with *The Love Machine,* which sold over 300,000 copies in hardcover. Michael Crichton's *The Andromeda Strain* launched a career on the bestseller list that would still be going strong over thirty years later.

Once again, there is an almost complete absence of conventional historical novels and romances (unless you can count Gwen Davis and Jackie Susann as romantic writers, which is a stretch). Hardcover publishers had more or less given up in these areas, in favor of more shocking novels, and were therefore—as usual—surprised when they bounced back again, as things always do in time.

A look at the bestseller lists of the sixties makes strange reading today for one who was in the industry then—and perhaps, in retrospect, at the peak of my career. The big stories of the decade were the election and the assassination of JFK, which produced a whole slew of books, the rise of the youth movement (represented on the list only by Lennon and McKuen), the long, agonizing march toward civil rights (which produced no books at all on the list), the Vietnam protests and the sharp division between the two generations that would lead Johnson not to seek re-election in 1968, and, in reaction, the election of Nixon and the re-escalation of the war in 1969 (which, again, produced no bestsellers). The answer, I think, is that those who were marching in the civil rights movement and those who were active against the war had no time to write books, and those who were on the side-lines, like book publishers, were too traumatized by the events to figure out what kind of books would sell. By and large, most editors in book publishing were antiwar, to one degree or another, while the publishers were mostly more cautious and willing, at least, to take the Johnson administration's views seriously. Thus, the protests in the streets were very often reflected by milder conflict between the generations in book publishing houses. I remember that I caused a major flap by publishing a fairly harmless book by the *Venceremos* Brigade—Americans who had gone to Cuba to help harvest sug-arcane—and that the National Book Award ceremonies were disrupted by angry protestors, many of them people I knew. On the subject of civil rights, the absence of bestselling books is also strange. It may derive in part from a degree of embarrassment on the part of publishers, most of whom were sym-pathetic to the civil rights movement, but at the same time only too aware that the few blacks who were employed in book publishing were still mostly in the mail room, not on editors row. Whatever the reason, the bestseller lists of the sixties have some curious holes in them when one considers what was going on in the country, and show some sign that a lot of people were busy buying cookbooks while the house burned.

1960

FICTION

1. *Advise and Consent,* by Allen Drury. Doubleday

2. *Hawaii,* by James A. Michener. Random House

3. *The Leopard,* by Giuseppe di Lampedusa. Pantheon Books

4. *The Chapman Report,* by Irving Wallace. Simon & Schuster

5. *Ourselves to Know,* by John O' Hara. Random House

6. *The Constant Image,* by Marcia Davenport. Scribner

7. *The Lovely Ambition,* by Mary Ellen Chase. Norton

8. *The Listener,* by Taylor Caldwell. Doubleday

9. *Trustee from the Toolroom,* by Nevil Shute. Morrow

10. *Sermons and Soda-Water,* by John O'Hara. Random House

NONFICTION

1. *Folk Medicine,* by D. C. Jarvis. Holt, Rinehart & Winston

2. *Better Homes and Gardens First Aid for Your Family.* Meredith Publishing Co.

3. *The General Foods Kitchens Cookbook.* Random House

4. *May This House Be Safe from Tigers,* by Alexander King. Simon & Schuster

5. *Better Homes and Gardens Dessert Book.* Meredith Publishing Co.

6. *Better Homes and Gardens Decorating Ideas.* Meredith Publishing Co.

7. *The Rise and Fall of the Third Reich,* by William L. Shirer. Simon & Schuster

8. *The Conscience of a Conservative,* by Barry Goldwater. Victor Publishing Co.

9. *I Kid You Not,* by Jack Paar. Little, Brown

10. *Between You, Me and the Gatepost,* by Pat Boone. Prentice-Hall

1961

FICTION

1. *The Agony and the Ecstasy,* by Irving Stone. Doubleday

2. *Franny and Zooey,* by J. D. Salinger. Little, Brown

3. *To Kill a Mockingbird,* by Harper Lee. Lippincott

4. *Mila 18,* by Leon Uris. Doubleday

5. *The Carpetbaggers,* by Harold Robbins. Simon & Schuster

6. *Tropic of Cancer,* by Henry Miller. Grove Press

7. *Winnie Ille Pu,* translated by Alexander Lenard. Dutton

8. *Daughter of Silence,* by Morris West. Morrow

9. *The Edge of Sadness,* by Edwin O'Connor. Little, Brown

10. *The Winter of Our Discontent,* by John Steinbeck. Viking Press

NONFICTION

1. *The New English Bible: The New Testament.* Cambridge University Press and Oxford University Press

2. *The Rise and Fall of the Third Reich,* by William Shirer. Simon & Schuster

3. *Better Homes and Gardens Sewing Book.* Meredith Publishing Co.

4. *Casserole Cook Book.* Meredith Publishing Co.

5. *A Nation of Sheep,* by William Lederer. Norton

6. *Better Homes and Gardens Nutrition for Your Family.* Meredith Publishing Co.

7. *The Making of the President, 1960,* by Theodore H. White. Atheneum Press

8. *Calories Don't Count,* by Dr. Herman Taller. Simon & Schuster

9. *Betty Crocker's New Picture Cook Book: New Edition.* McGraw-Hill

10. *Ring of Bright Water,* by Gavin Maxwell. Dutton

1962

FICTION

1. *Ship of Fools,* by Katherine Anne Porter. Little, Brown

2. *Dearly Beloved,* by Anne Morrow Lindbergh. Harcourt, Brace & World

3. *A Shade of Difference,* by Allen Drury. Doubleday

4. *Youngblood Hawke,* by Herman Wouk. Doubleday

5. *Franny and Zooey,* by J. D. Salinger. Little, Brown

6. *Fail-Safe,* by Eugene Burdick and Harvey Wheeler. McGraw-Hill

7. *Seven Days in May,* by Fletcher Knebel and Charles W. Bailey II.

   Harper & Row

8. *The Prize,* by Irving Wallace. Simon & Schuster

9. *The Agony and the Ecstasy,* by Irving Stone. Doubleday

10. *The Reivers,* by William Faulkner. Random House

NONFICTION

1. *Calories Don't Count,* by D. Herman Taller. Simon & Schuster

2. *The New English Bible: The New Testament.* Cambridge University Press
   and Oxford University Press

3. *Better Homes and Gardens Cook Book: New Edition.* Meredith
   Publishing Co.

4. *O Ye Jigs & Juleps!* by Virginia Cary Hudson. Macmillan

5. *Happiness Is a Warm Puppy,* by Charles M. Schulz. Determined Productions

6. *The Joy of Cooking: New Edition,* by Irma S. Rombauer and Marion
   Rombauer Becker. Bobbs-Merrill

7. *My Life in Court,* by Louis Nizer. Doubleday

8. *The Rothschilds,* by Frederic Morton. Atheneum Publishers

9. *Sex and the Single Girl,* by Helen Gurley Brown. Bernard Geis

10. *Travels with Charley,* by John Steinbeck. Viking Press

1963

FICTION

1. *The Shoes of the Fisherman,* by Morris L. West. Morrow

2. *The Group,* by Mary McCarthy. Harcourt, Brace & World

3. *Raise High the Roof Beam, Carpenters, and Seymour—An Introduction,* by J. D. Salinger. Little, Brown

4. *Caravans,* by James A. Michener. Random House

5. *Elizabeth Appleton,* by John O'Hara. Random House

6. *Grandmother and the Priests,* by Taylor Caldwell. Doubleday

7. *City of Night,* by John Rechy. Grove Press

8. *The Glass-Blowers,* by Daphne du Maurier. Doubleday

9. *The Sand Pebbles,* by Richard McKenna. Harper & Row

10. *The Battle of the Villa Fiorita,* by Rumer Godden. Viking Press

NONFICTION

1. *Happiness Is a Warm Puppy,* by Charles M. Schulz. Determined Productions

2. *Security Is a Thumb and a Blanket,* by Charles M. Schulz. Determined Productions

3. *J. F. K.: The Man and the Myth,* by Victor Lasky. Macmillan

4. *Profiles in Courage: Inaugural Edition,* by John F. Kennedy. Harper & Row

5. *O Ye Jigs & Juleps!* by Virginia Cary Hudson. Macmillan

6. *Better Homes and Gardens Bread Cook Book.* Meredith Publishing Co.

7. *The Pillsbury Family Cookbook.* Harper & Row

8. *I Owe Russia $1200,* by Bob Hope. Doubleday

9. *Heloise's Housekeeping Hints.* Prentice-Hall

10. *Better Homes and Gardens Baby Book.* Meredith Publishing Co.

1964

FICTION

1. *The Spy Who Came in From the Cold,* by John le Carré. Coward-McCann

2. *Candy,* by Terry Southern and Mason Hoffenberg. Putnam

3. *Herzog,* by Saul Bellow. Viking Press

4. *Armageddon,* by Leon Uris. Doubleday

5. *The Man,* by Irving Wallace. Simon & Schuster

6. *The Rector of Justin,* by Louis Auchincloss. Houghton Mifflin

7. *The Martyred,* by Richard E. Kim. Braziller

8. *You Only Live Twice,* by Ian Fleming. New American Library

9. *This Rough Magic,* by Mary Stewart. Morrow

10. *Convention,* by Fletcher Knebel and Charles W. Bailey II. Harper & Row

NONFICTION

1. *Four Days,* by American Heritage and United Press International. Simon & Schuster

2. *I Need All the Friends I Can Get,* by Charles M. Schulz. Determined Productions

3. *Profiles in Courage: Memorial Edition,* by John F. Kennedy. Harper & Row

4. *In His Own Write,* by John Lennon. Simon & Schuster

5. *Christmas Is Together-Time,* by Charles M. Schulz. Determined Productions

6. *A Day in the Life of President Kennedy,* by Jim Bishop. Random House

7. *The Kennedy Wit,* compiled by Bill Adler. Citadel Press

8. *A Moveable Feast,* by Ernest Hemingway. Scribner

9. *Reminiscences,* by General Douglas MacArthur. McGraw-Hill

10. *The John F. Kennedys,* by Mark Shaw. Farrar, Straus & Giroux

1965

FICTION

1. *The Source,* by James A. Michener. Random House

2. *Up the Down Staircase,* by Bel Kaufman. Prentice-Hall

3. *Herzog,* by Saul Bellow. Viking Press

4. *The Looking Glass War,* by John le Carré. Coward-McCann

5. *The Green Berets,* by Robin Moore. Crown

6. *Those Who Love,* by Irving Stone. Doubleday

7. *The Man with the Golden Gun,* by Ian Fleming. New American Library

8. *Hotel,* by Arthur Hailey. Doubleday

9. *The Ambassador,* by Morris West. Morrow

10. *Don't Stop the Carnival,* by Herman Wouk. Doubleday

NONFICTION

1. *How to Be a Jewish Mother,* by Dan Greenburg. Price/Stern/Sloan

2. *A Gift of Prophecy,* by Ruth Montgomery. Morrow

3. *Games People Play,* by Eric Berne, M. D. Grove Press

4. *World Aflame,* by Billy Graham. Doubleday

5. *Happiness Is a Dry Martini,* by Johnny Carson. Doubleday

6. *Markings,* by Dag Hammarskjöld. Knopf

7. *A Thousand Days,* by Arthur Schlesinger Jr. Houghton Mifflin

8. *My Shadow Ran Fast,* by Bill Sands. Prentice-Hall

9. *Kennedy,* by Theodore C. Sorensen. Harper & Row

10. *The Making of the President, 1964,* by Theodore H. White. Atheneum

1966

FICTION

1. *Valley of the Dolls,* by Jacqueline Susann. Bernard Geis

2. *The Adventurers,* by Harold Robbins. Trident Press

3. *The Secret of Santa Vittoria,* by Robert Crichton. Simon & Schuster

4. *Capable of Honor,* by Allen Drury. Doubleday

5. *The Double Image,* by Helen MacInnes. Harcourt, Brace & World

6. *The Fixer,* by Bernard Malamud. Farrar, Straus & Giroux

7. *Tell No Man,* by Adela Rogers St. Johns. Doubleday

8. *Tai-Pan,* by James Clavell. Atheneum Publishers

9. *The Embezzler,* by Louis Auchincloss. Houghton Mifflin

10. *All in the Family,* by Edwin O'Connor. Atlantic-Little, Brown

NONFICTION

1. *How to Avoid Probate,* by Norman F. Dacey. Crown

2. *Human Sexual Response,* by William Howard Masters and Virginia E. Johnston. Little, Brown

3. *In Cold Blood,* by Truman Capote. Random House

4. *Games People Play,* by Eric Berne, M. D. Grove Press

5. *A Thousand Days,* by Arthur M. Schlesinger Jr. Houghton Mifflin

6. *Everything But Money,* by Sam Levenson. Simon & Schuster

7. *The Random House Dictionary of the English Language.* Random House

8. *Rush to Judgment,* by Mark Lane. Holt, Rinehart & Winston

9. *The Last Battle,* by Cornelius Ryan. Simon & Schuster

10. *Phyllis Diller's Housekeeping Hints,* by Phyllis Diller. Doubleday

1967

FICTION

1. *The Arrangement,* by Elia Kazan. Stein & Day

2-3. *The Confessions of Nat Turner,* by William Styron. Random House

2-3. *The Chosen,* by Chaim Potok. Simon & Schuster

4. *Topaz,* by Leon Uris. McGraw-Hill

5. *Christy,* by Catherine Marshall. McGraw-Hill

6. *The Eighth Day,* by Thornton Wilder. Harper & Row

7. *Rosemary's Baby,* by Ira Levin. Random House

8. *The Plot,* by Irving Wallace. Simon & Schuster

9. *The Gabriel Hounds,* by Mary Stewart. Morrow

10. *The Exhibitionist,* by Henry Sutton. Bernard Geis

NONFICTION

1. *Death of a President,* by William Manchester. Harper & Row

2. *Misery Is a Blind Date,* by Johnny Carson. Doubleday

3. *Games People Play,* by Eric Berne, M. D. Grove Press

4. *Stanyan Street & Other Sorrows,* by Rod McKuen. Random House

5. *A Modern Priest Looks at His Outdated Church,* by Father James Kavanaugh. Trident Press

6. *Everything but Money,* by Sam Levenson. Simon & Schuster

7. *Our Crowd,* by Stephen Birmingham. Harper & Row

8-9-10. *Edgar Cayce—The Sleeping Prophet,* by Jess Stern. Doubleday

8-9-10. *Better Homes and Gardens Favorite Ways with Chicken.* Meredith Press

8-9-10. *Phyllis Diller's Marriage Manual,* by Phyllis Diller. Doubleday

1968

FICTION

1. *Airport,* by Arthur Hailey. Doubleday

2. *Couples,* by John Updike. Knopf

3. *The Salzburg Connection,* by Helen MacInnes. Harcourt, Brace & World

4. *A Small Town in Germany,* by John le Carré. Coward-McCann

5. *Testimony of Two Men,* by Taylor Caldwell. Doubleday

6. *Preserve and Protect,* by Allen Drury. Doubleday

7. *Myra Breckinridge,* by Gore Vidal. Little, Brown

8. *Vanished,* by Fletcher Knebel. Doubleday

9. *Christy,* by Catherine Marshall. McGraw-Hill

10. *The Tower of Babel,* by Morris L. West. Morrow

NONFICTION

1. *Better Homes and Gardens New Cook Book.* Meredith Press

2. *The Random House Dictionary of the English Language: College Edition.* Editor-in-chief Laurence Urdang. Random House

3. *Listen to the Warm,* by Rod McKuen. Random House

4. *Between Parent and Child,* by Haim G. Ginott. Macmillan

5. *Lonesome Cities,* by Rod McKuen. Random House

6. *The Doctor's Quick Weight Loss Diet,* by Erwin M. Stillman and Samm Sinclair Baker. Prentice-Hall

7. *The Money Game,* by Adam Smith. Random House

8. *Stanyan Street & Other Sorrows,* by Rod McKuen. Random House

9. *The Weight Watchers Cook Book,* by Jean Nidetch. Hearthside Press

10. *Better Homes and Gardens Eat and Stay Slim.* Meredith Press

1969

FICTION

1. *Portnoy's Complaint,* by Philip Roth. Random House

2. *The Godfather,* by Mario Puzo. Putnam

3. *The Love Machine,* by Jacqueline Susann. Simon & Schuster

4. *The Inheritors,* by Harold Robbins. Trident Press

5. *The Andromeda Strain,* by Michael Crichton. Knopf

6. *The Seven Minutes,* by Irving Wallace. Simon & Schuster

7. *Naked Came the Stranger,* by Penelope Ashe. Lyle Stuart

8. *The Promise,* by Chaim Potok. Knopf

9. *The Pretenders,* by Gwen Davis. World Publishing Co.

10. *The House on the Strand,* by Daphne du Maurier. Doubleday

NONFICTION

1. *American Heritage Dictionary of the English Language,* editor-in-chief
   William Morris. Houghton Mifflin

2. *In Someone's Shadow,* by Rod McKuen. Random House

3. *The Peter Principle,* by Laurence J. Peter and Raymond Hull. Morrow

4. *Between Parent and Teenager,* by Dr. Haim G. Ginott. Macmillan

5. *The Graham Kerr Cookbook,* by the Galloping Gourmet. Doubleday

6. *The Selling of the President 1968,* by Joe McGinniss. Trident Press

7. *Miss Craig's 21-Day Shape-Up Program for Men and Women,* by
   Marjorie Craig. Random House

8. *My Life and Prophecies,* by Jeane Dixon with René Noorbergen. Morrow

9. *Linda Goodman's Sun Signs,* by Linda Goodman. Taplinger

10. *Twelve Years of Christmas,* by Rod McKuen. Random House

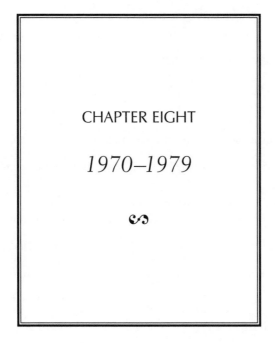

CHAPTER EIGHT

1970–1979

☙

A N ASTUTE PUBLISHER might have guessed it, but "as the flames climbed high into the night / To light the sacrificial rite"—the Vietnam War was at its peak—an element of good old-fashioned romance was coming back onto the list again, with Erich Segal's *Love Story*, John Fowles's *The French Lieutenant's Woman*, and the reappearance of familiar romantic fiction with Victoria Holt's *The Secret Woman*. Just when you thought it was all going to be rough sex and big-subject novels, here is Victoria Holt, not to speak of Erich Segal at #1, with perhaps the drippiest line in the history of sentimental fiction, "Love means never having to say you're sorry." The best-seller list has always been like that. The moment you kiss a category or a genre good-bye, there it is, back again on the list, usually in some slightly new form, but always perfectly recognizable as the return of yesterday's hot item. It's as if buggy whips came back into fashion from time to time, and is one of the many things that makes selling books different from selling other things.

Publishers who had been flogging their editors on in search of Jackie Susann write-alikes, now had to back off and look for big romantic novels, in imitation of Victoria Holt, or flew to England hoping to find another John Fowles. In nonfiction two more books of poetry by Rod McKuen made the list, together with—catch the irony of this!—*Better Homes and Gardens Fondue and Tabletop Cooking, The Sensuous Woman*, by "J.," and, at #1, *Everything You Always Wanted to Know about Sex, but Were Afraid to Ask,* by David Reuben, M.D.

Better sex, more sex, plus tabletop cooking, says something about the priorities of Americans in the first year of Richard Nixon's presidency, or at any rate the ones who were buying books. People were looking for domestic happiness, in retreat from the bruising ethical, moral, and political conflicts of the sixties, in a mood to get the war over with and enjoy life—which perhaps explains why so many of them turned angry as the war escalated instead. The same strain of sensual and romantic writing that had suddenly reappeared on the fiction bestseller list was now appearing on the nonfiction list.

For those who didn't get the message, 1971 reinforced it—*The Sensuous Man*; the *Better Homes and Gardens Blender Cook Book*; *Any Woman Can!* (an encouraging guide to female orgasm); another book of poetry by Rod McKuen; and *I'm O.K., You're O.K.,* the granddaddy of an endless line of "feel-good" self-help books, which professed to tell the reader, in effect, to chill out and calm down and begin to like himself or herself the way he or she was, rather than change to meet the rest of the world's expectations. Blender cooking and orgasm—*voilà les années* 1970.

1972 was a clone—*Open Marriage* (does anybody remember that prescriptive self-help relationship book, and is anybody married to the same person they were when they read it and followed its advice?), *Better Homes and Gardens Menu Cook Book, Dr. Atkins' Diet Revolution, Better Homes and Gardens Low-Calorie Desserts, The Peter Prescription!* Self-improvement (and self-indulgence in everything but calories) up the gazoo, as people used to say at the time! On the other hand, my friend and author Carlos Castaneda hit the year's list with *Journey to Ixtlan,* perhaps his best book, though a lot of people who bought it probably thought it was about getting the maximum bang from a joint. In fiction, *Jonathan Livingston Seagull,* which sold nearly 2 million copies in hardcover, was #1, but the best book on the list by a long shot was Frederick Forsyth's great thriller *The Day of the Jackal,* which can still be read with pleasure today.

In 1973, Jacqueline Susann hit the list with *Once Is Not Enough*—she had left S&S angrily, and our president, Richard E. Snyder, sent her one rose on publication, with the memorable card: "For us, once was plenty."

Otherwise *Jonathan Livingston Seagull* was #1 for a second year, while the rest of the list, with the exception of Mary Stewart, was mostly written by men: Kurt Vonnegut Jr., Frederick Forsyth, Gore Vidal, Irwin Shaw, Robert Ludlum, Paul E. Erdman, Graham Greene. Gore Vidal's *Burr* is a book that has stood the test of time, as have Graham Greene's *The Honorary Consul* and perhaps Kurt Vonnegut's *Breakfast of Champions*. On the whole a good year for fiction.

Nonfiction brought a bumper crop of feel-good books. On the psychological front, *I'm O.K., You're O.K.* (for the second year), *The Joy of Sex*, and *How to Be Your Own Best Friend*. On the practical side, *Dr. Atkins' Diet Revolution* (for the second year), *Weight Watchers Program Cookbook*, and *Better Homes and Gardens Home Canning Cook Book*.

This pattern would be repeated in 1974—*huge* novels, including Michener's *Centennial*, Richard Adams's *Watership Down*, Peter Benchley's *Jaws*, Harold Robbins's *The Pirate*, and a nonfiction list that says everything about life in the mid-1970s, including Marabel Morgan's *The Total Woman* (at #1), a sequel to *The Joy of Sex*, and Harry Browne's *You Can Profit from a Monetary Crisis*.

1975 brought the same again—big novels, including *Ragtime, Looking for Mister Goodbar*, and *Shogun*, not much in the way of women's fiction, and a nonfiction list that reads like a prescription for better health and living: *TM: Discovering Energy and Overcoming Stress; Total Fitness in 30 Minutes a Week; The Save-Your-Life Diet*. Remember TM? Remember the Beatles' guru, the Maharishi Mahesh Yogi? Remember Sufis? For those interested in charting the spiritual journey of Americans in the third quarter of the twentieth century, the bestseller list is a good place to start. Americans were determined to be fit, thin, sexually fulfilled, relaxed, successful, and at peace with themselves—a tall order, one might think, but one in the cause of which a lot of bestsellers were published, and no doubt read, not many of which, I would guess, are still being read today. Hardly anything dates more quickly than yesterday's self-help books, or seems more old-fashioned a couple of decades down the road.

Of course the Nixon resignation created numerous bestsellers, notable among then *All the President's Men* (1974), *The Final Days* (1976), and *Blind Ambition* (1976), and created a mini-industry of Watergate books and memoirs that would sustain publishers for the rest of the decade. Hardly anybody involved in the Watergate crisis, on either side, passed up the chance to write about it, and it would be possible to collect a substantial library on the subject. Four of the ten nonfiction books on the 1976 bestseller list are about Watergate—those that aren't about Watergate include *Your Erroneous Zones*; *The Hite Report: A Nationwide Study of Female Sexuality*; and *Passages*—once again, all "lifestyle" books.

1977 was the year of *The Thorn Birds,* signaling the return of big romantic fiction in a big way, which sold an astonishing 600,000 copies, and in nonfiction of *Roots,* which sold nearly 800,000 copies. Both went on to become hugely successful television miniseries and to sell millions of copies in paperback. 1978 was the year of Judith Krantz's *Scruples,* which made it clear that the big women's novel was back and here to stay for a while. Nonfiction showed not only the waning of interest in Watergate (though Nixon's own memoirs made the list at #6), but also the beginning of a renewed interest in personal scandal and the celebrity cult, exemplified by Kitty Kelley's *Jackie Oh!,* the first radical deconstruction of the Jacqueline Kennedy–fairy-princess myth, and *Mommie Dearest,* Christina Crawford's far more brutal deconstruction of her mother, movie star Joan Crawford (almost everybody remembers the famous wire coat hanger story).

1978 was also the year in which Americans started to run in large numbers, marked by the huge sale of James Fixx's *The Complete Book of Running,* which was a perfect example of a book that not only coincided with, but perhaps even started, a long running craze. I actually met Fixx on a talk show in Chicago, where to my astonishment, he fainted on camera as his interview began. At first, I thought that Fixx was a poor example of his own recommendations for physical fitness, but it turned out that he suffered from severe stage fright, and at the very start of his author's tour, wasn't ready for the camera.

1979, believe it or not, marked the debut of Stephen King on the yearly list with *The Dead Zone,* still going strong twenty years later, though the most notable work of fiction on the list was undoubtedly William Styron's *Sophie's Choice.* The nonfiction list continued to demonstrate the American public's determination to find life improvement and enhancement in the bookstore: *The Complete Scarsdale Medical Diet* (the author, Dr. Herman Tarnower, was to find even greater fame when he was shot to death by his mistress, Jean Harris, some years later), *How to Prosper During the Coming Bad Years, The Pritikin Program for Diet and Exercise, How to Become Financially Independent by Investing in Real Estate,* and *The Fannie Farmer Cookbook.*

It should be noted that, at this stage, hardcover nonfiction still generally outsold fiction by a substantial margin. Most of the novels at the top of the list sold under 250,000 in hardcover, whereas Dr. Tarnower's diet book sold nearly 700,000 copies. Also mass-market sales were still huge. *The Thorn Birds* sold 7,450,000 copies in paperback, *Scruples* over 4 million. By and large, in mass market, the ratio between fiction and nonfiction was reversed—it was the fiction that sold in the really large numbers.

The trend in bookstores was toward the "mall stores" during the seventies. As the suburban shopping mall became larger and more upmarket—most soon contained a multiplex movie theater, restaurants, coffee shops, fashion brand-name stores—the move to put bookstores in there was irresistible, and, for a time, seemed to revolutionize the business of selling books. Here, after all, were huge numbers of people, most of whom had never been in a bookstore, and an opportunity to sell books at night and on the weekends, when people had the time and the incentive to shop. Book sales started to rise, while at the same time, the gradual erosion of the smaller, "independent" bookstores, most of which were situated in what was fast becoming the "dead ground" of urban, inner-city shopping areas, became irreversible, leading to the extinction of many old and distinguished bookshops. The "chain stores" had the capital to go where the customers were, and to invent a new kind of bookselling that was tailored to mall shoppers—high visibility, lots of displays, open space, the kind of store that could exist and make money next to Victoria's Secret or the Gap. This had its advantages for publishers, if you only looked at the numbers, but it brought about real problems where the kind of books that the independents knew how to sell "by hand," to special customers, were concerned. One consequence was an increasing reluctance of publishers to back "difficult" or "special" books, in favor of big bestsellers, with the result that buying the big "brand-name" authors became a ruinously expensive and risky proposition; another was the decline in book club membership as the kind of people who had once belonged to them found they could buy the books they wanted just as cheaply, or cheaper, at a shopping mall, and drive home with their purchases, rather than wait for them to arrive by mail—instant gratification.

1970

—•◦•—

FICTION

1. *Love Story,* by Erich Segal. Harper & Row

2. *The French Lieutenant's Woman,* by John Fowles. Little, Brown

3. *Islands in the Stream,* by Ernest Hemingway. Scribner

4. *The Crystal Cave,* by Mary Stewart. Morrow

5. *Great Lion of God,* by Taylor Caldwell. Doubleday

6. *QB VII,* by Leon Uris. Doubleday

7. *The Gang That Couldn't Shoot Straight,* by Jimmy Breslin. Viking Press

8. *The Secret Woman,* by Victoria Holt. Doubleday

9. *Travels with My Aunt,* by Graham Greene. Viking Press

10. *Rich Man, Poor Man,* by Irwin Shaw. Delacorte Press

NONFICTION

1. *Everything You Always Wanted to Know about Sex, but Were Afraid to Ask,* by David Reuben, M. D. McKay

2. *The New English Bible.* Oxford University Press and Cambridge University Press

3. *The Sensuous Woman,* by "J." Lyle Stuart

4. *Better Homes and Gardens Fondue and Tabletop Cooking.* Meredith

5. *Up the Organization,* by Robert Townsend. Knopf

6. *Ball Four,* by Jim Bouton. World Publishing Co.

7. *American Heritage Dictionary of the English Language,* editor-in-chief William Morris. Houghton Mifflin

8. *Body Language,* by Julius Fast. M. Evans

9. *In Someone's Shadow,* by Rod McKuen. Random House

10. *Caught in the Quiet,* by Rod McKuen. Random House Stanyan Books

1971

FICTION

1. *Wheels,* by Arthur Hailey. Doubleday

2. *The Exorcist,* by William P. Blatty. Harper & Row

3. *The Passions of the Mind,* by Irving Stone. Doubleday

4. *The Day of the Jackal,* by Frederick Forsyth. Viking Press

5. *The Betsy,* by Harold Robbins. Trident Press

6. *Message from Malaga,* by Helen MacInnes. Harcourt Brace Jovanovich

7. *The Winds of War,* by Herman Wouk. Little, Brown

8. *The Drifters,* by James A. Michener. Random House

9. *The Other,* by Thomas Tryon. Knopf

10. *Rabbit Redux,* by John Updike. Knopf

NONFICTION

1. *The Sensuous Man,* by "M." Lyle Stuart

2. *Bury My Heart at Wounded Knee,* by Dee Brown. Holt, Rinehart & Winston

3. *Better Homes and Gardens Blender Cook Book.* Meredith

4. *I'm O. K., You're O. K.,* by Thomas Harris. Harper & Row

5. *Any Woman Can!* by David Reuben, M. D., McKay

6. *Inside the Third Reich,* by Albert Speer. Macmillan

7. *Eleanor and Franklin,* by Joseph P. Lash. Norton

8. *Wunnerful, Wunnerful!* by Lawrence Welk. Prentice-Hall

9. *Honor Thy Father,* by Gay Talese. World

10. *Fields of Wonder,* by Rod McKuen. Random House

1972

FICTION

1. *Jonathan Livingston Seagull,* by Richard Bach. Macmillan

2. *August, 1914,* by Alexander Solzhenitsyn. Farrar, Straus & Giroux

3. *The Odessa File,* by Frederick Forsyth. Viking

4. *The Day of the Jackal,* by Frederick Forsyth. Viking

5. *The Word,* by Irving Wallace. Simon & Schuster

6. *The Winds of War,* by Herman Wouk. Little, Brown

7. *Captains and the Kings,* by Taylor Caldwell. Doubleday

8. *Two from Galilee,* by Marjorie Holmes. Revell

9. *My Name Is Asher Lev,* by Chaim Potok. Knopf

10. *Semi-Tough,* by Dan Jenkins. Atheneum

NONFICTION

1. *The Living Bible,* by Kenneth Taylor. Doubleday

2. *I'm O. K., You're O. K.,* by Thomas Harris. Harper & Row

3. *Open Marriage,* by Nena and George O'Neill. M. Evans

4. *Harry S. Truman,* by Margaret Truman. Morrow

5. *Dr. Atkins' Diet Revolution,* by Robert C. Atkins. McKay

6. *Better Homes and Gardens Menu Cook Book.* Meredith

7. *The Peter Prescription,* by Laurence J. Peter. Morrow

8. *A World Beyond,* by Ruth Montgomery. Coward, McCann & Geoghegan

9. *Journey to Ixtlan,* by Carlos Castaneda. Simon & Schuster

10. *Better Homes and Gardens Low-Calorie Desserts.* Meredith

1973

FICTION

1. *Jonathan Livingston Seagull,* by Richard Bach. Macmillan

2. *Once Is Not Enough,* by Jacqueline Susann. Morrow

3. *Breakfast of Champions,* by Kurt Vonnegut Jr. Delacorte/Lawrence

4. *The Odessa File,* by Frederick Forsyth. Viking

5. *Burr,* by Gore Vidal. Random House

6. *The Hollow Hills,* by Mary Stewart. Morrow

7. *Evening in Byzantium,* by Irwin Shaw. Delacorte

8. *The Matlock Paper,* by Robert Ludlum. Dial Press

9. *The Billion Dollar Sure Thing,* by Paul E. Erdman. Scribner

10. *The Honorary Consul,* by Graham Greene. Simon & Schuster

NONFICTION

1. *The Living Bible,* by Kenneth Taylor. Doubleday and Tyndale House

2. *Dr. Atkins' Diet Revolution,* by Robert C. Atkins. McKay

3. *I'm O. K., You're O. K.,* by Thomas Harris. Harper & Row

4. *The Joy of Sex,* by Alex Comfort. Crown

5. *Weight Watchers® Program Cookbook,* by Jean Nidetch. Hearthside Press

6. *How to Be Your Own Best Friend,* by Mildred Newman et al. Random House

7. *The Art of Walt Disney,* by Christopher Finch. Harry N. Abrams

8. *Better Homes and Gardens Home Canning Cook Book.* Meredith

9. *Alistair Cooke's America,* by Alistair Cooke. Knopf

10. *Sybil,* by Flora R. Schreiber. Regnery

1974

FICTION

1. *Centennial,* by James A. Michener. Random House

2. *Watership Down,* by Richard Adams. Macmillan

3. *Jaws,* by Peter Benchley. Doubleday

4. *Tinker, Tailor, Soldier, Spy,* by John le Carré. Knopf

5. *Something Happened,* by Joseph Heller. Knopf

6. *The Dogs of War,* by Frederick Forsyth. Viking

7. *The Pirate,* by Harold J. Robbins. Simon & Schuster

8. *I Heard the Owl Call My Name,* by Margaret Craven. Doubleday

9. *The Seven-Per-Cent Solution,* by John H. Watson, M. D., as edited by Nicholas Meyer. Dutton

10. *The Fan Club,* by Irving Wallace. Simon & Schuster

NONFICTION

1. *The Total Woman,* by Marabel Morgan. Revell

2. *All the President's Men,* by Carl Bernstein and Bob Woodward. Simon & Schuster

3. *Plain Speaking: An Oral Biography of Harry S. Truman,* by Merle Miller. Putnam

4. *More Joy: A Lovemaking Companion to The Joy of Sex,* ed. by Alex Comfort. Crown

5. *Alistair Cooke's America,* by Alistair Cooke. Knopf

6. *Tales of Power,* by Carlos A. Castaneda. Simon & Schuster

7. *You Can Profit from a Monetary Crisis,* by Harry Browne. Macmillan

8. *All Things Bright and Beautiful,* by James Herriot. St. Martin's

9. *The Bermuda Triangle,* by Charles Berlitz with J. Manson Valentine. Doubleday

10. *The Memory Book,* by Harry Lorayne and Jerry Lucas. Stein & Day

1975

FICTION

1. *Ragtime,* by E. L. Doctorow. Random House

2. *The Moneychangers,* by Arthur Hailey. Doubleday

3. *Curtain,* by Agatha Christie. Dodd, Mead

4. *Looking for Mister Goodbar,* by Judith Rossner. Simon & Schuster

5. *The Choirboys,* by Joseph Wambaugh. Delacorte

6. *The Eagle Has Landed,* by Jack Higgins. Holt, Rinehart and Winston

7. *The Greek Treasure: A Biographical Novel of Henry and Sophia Schliemann,* by Irving Stone. Doubleday

8. *The Great Train Robbery,* by Michael Crichton. Knopf

9. *Shogun,* by James Clavell. Atheneum

10. *Humboldt's Gift,* by Saul Bellow. Viking

NONFICTION

1. *Angels: God's Secret Agents,* by Billy Graham. Doubleday

2. *Winning Through Intimidation,* by Robert Ringer. Funk & Wagnalls

3. *TM: Discovering Energy and Overcoming Stress,* by Harold H. Bloomfield. Delacorte

4. *The Ascent of Man,* by Jacob Bronowski. Little, Brown

5. *Sylvia Porter's Money Book,* by Sylvia Porter. Doubleday

6. *Total Fitness in 30 Minutes a Week,* by Laurence E. Morehouse

7. *The Bermuda Triangle,* by Charles Berlitz with J. Manson Valentine. Doubleday

8. *The Save-Your-Life Diet,* by David Reuben. Random House

9. *Bring on the Empty Horses,* by David Niven. Putnam

10. *Breach of Faith: The Fall of Richard Nixon,* by Theodore H. White. Atheneum/Reader's Digest Press

1976

FICTION

1. *Trinity,* by Leon Uris. Doubleday

2. *Sleeping Murder,* by Agatha Christie. Dodd, Mead

3. *Dolores,* by Jacqueline Susann. Morrow

4. *Storm Warning,* by Jack Higgins. Holt, Rinehart & Winston

5. *The Deep,* by Peter Benchley. Doubleday

6. *1876,* by Gore Vidal. Random House

7. *Slapstick or Lonesome No More!* by Kurt Vonnegut Jr. Delacorte/
   Seymour Lawrence

8. *The Lonely Lady,* by Harold Robbins. Simon & Schuster

9. *Touch Not the Cat,* by Mary Stewart. Morrow

10. *A Stranger in the Mirror,* by Sidney Sheldon. Morrow

NONFICTION

1. *The Final Days,* by Bob Woodward and Carl Bernstein. Simon & Schuster

2. *Roots,* by Alex Haley. Doubleday

3. *Your Erroneous Zones,* by Dr. Wayne W. Dyer. Funk & Wagnalls

4. *Passages: The Predictable Crises of Adult Life,* by Gail Sheehy. E. P. Dutton

5. *Born Again,* by Charles W. Colson. Chosen Books

6. *The Grass Is Always Greener over the Septic Tank,* by Erma Bombeck.
   McGraw-Hill

7. *Angels: God's Secret Agents,* by Billy Graham. Doubleday

8. *Blind Ambition: The White House Years,* by John Dean. Simon & Schuster

9. *The Hite Report: A Nationwide Study of Female Sexuality,* by Shere Hite.
   Macmillan

10. *The Right and the Power: The Prosecution of Watergate,* by Leon Jaworski.
    Reader's Digest Press/Gulf Publishing

1977

FICTION

1. *The Silmarillion,* by J. R. R. Tolkien; ed. by Christopher Tolkien. Houghton Mifflin

2. *The Thorn Birds,* by Colleen McCullough. Harper & Row

3. *Illusions: The Adventures of a Reluctant Messiah,* by Richard Bach. Delacorte/Eleanor Friede

4. *The Honourable Schoolboy,* by John le Carré. Knopf

5. *Oliver's Story,* by Erich Segal. Harper & Row

6. *Dreams Die First,* by Harold Robbins. Simon & Schuster

7. *Beggarman, Thief,* by Irwin Shaw. Delacorte

8. *How to Save Your Own Life,* by Erica Jong. Holt, Rinehart & Winston

9. *Delta of Venus: Erotica,* by Anaïs Nin. Harcourt Brace Jovanovich

10. *Daniel Martin,* by John Fowles. Little, Brown

NONFICTION

1. *Roots,* by Alex Haley. Doubleday

2. *Looking Out for #1,* by Robert Ringer. Funk & Wagnalls

3. *All Things Wise and Wonderful,* by James Herriot. St. Martin's

4. *Your Erroneous Zones,* by Dr. Wayne W. Dyer. Funk & Wagnells

5. *The Book of Lists,* by David Wallechinsky, Irving Wallace and Amy Wallace. Morrow

6. *The Possible Dream: A Candid Look at Amway,* by Charles Paul Conn. Revell

7. *The Dragons of Eden: Speculations on the Evolution of Human Intelligence,* by Carl Sagan. Random House

8. *The Second Ring of Power,* by Carlos Castaneda. Simon & Schuster

9. *The Grass Is Always Greener over the Septic Tank,* by Erma Bombeck McGraw-Hill

10. *The Amityville Horror,* by Jay Anson. Prentice-Hall

1978

FICTION

1. *Chesapeake,* by James A. Michener. Random House

2. *War and Remembrance,* by Herman Wouk. Little, Brown

3. *Fools Die,* by Mario Puzo. Putnam

4. *Bloodlines,* by Sidney Sheldon. Morrow

5. *Scruples,* by Judith Krantz. Crown

6. *Evergreen,* by Belva Plain. Delacorte

7. *Illusions: The Adventures of a Reluctant Messiah,* by Richard Bach. Delacorte/Eleanor Friede

8. *The Holcroft Covenant,* by Robert Ludlum. Richard Marek

9. *Second Generation,* by Howard Fast. Houghton Mifflin

10. *Eye of the Needle,* by Ken Follett. Arbor House

11. *The Human Factor,* by Graham Greene. Simon & Schuster

12. *The Far Pavilions,* by M. M. Kaye. St. Martin's

13. *Prelude to Terror,* by Helen MacInnes. Harcourt Brace Jovanovich

14. *The World According to Garp,* by John Irving. Dutton/Robbins

15. *Whistle,* by James Jones. Delacorte

NONFICTION

1. *If Life Is a Bowl of Cherries—What Am I Doing in the Pits?* by Erma Bombeck. McGraw-Hill

2. *Gnomes,* by Wil Huygen with illustrations by Rien Poortvliet. Abrams

3. *The Complete Book of Running,* by James Fixx. Random House

4. *Mommie Dearest,* by Christina Crawford. Morrow

5. *Pulling Your Own Strings,* by Dr. Wayne W. Dyer. T. Y. Crowell

6. *The Memoirs of Richard Nixon,* by Richard Nixon. Grosset & Dunlap

7. *A Distant Mirror: The Calamitous Fourteenth Century,* by Barbara W. Tuchman. Knopf

8. *Faeries,* described and illustrated by Brian Froud and Alan Lee. Abrams

9. *In Search of History: A Personal Adventure,* by Theodore H. White. Harper & Row

10. *The Muppet Show Book,* by The Muppet People. Abrams

11. *The Ends of Power,* by H. R. Haldeman. Times Books

12. *My Mother/My Self: A Daughter's Search for Identity*, by Nancy Friday. Delacorte

13. *American Caesar: Douglas MacArthur, 1880–1964*, by William Manchester. Little, Brown

14. *A Time for Truth*, by William E. Simon. Reader's Digest

15. *Jackie Oh!,* by Kitty Kelley. Lyle Stuart

1979

FICTION

1. *The Matarese Circle,* by Robert Ludlum. Richard Marek

2. *Sophie's Choice,* by William Styron. Random House

3. *Overload,* by Arthur Hailey. Doubleday

4. *Memories of Another Day,* by Harold Robbins. Simon & Schuster

5. *Jailbird,* by Kurt Vonnegut Jr. Delacorte Press/Seymour Lawrence

6. *The Dead Zone,* by Stephen King. Viking

7. *The Last Enchantment,* by Mary Stewart. Morrow

8. *The Establishment,* by Howard Fast. Houghton Mifflin

9. *The Third World War: August 1985,* by General Sir John Hackett, et al. Macmillan

10. *Smiley's People,* by John le Carré. Knopf

11. *Triple,* by Ken Follett. Arbor House

12. *Good as Gold,* by Joseph Heller. Simon & Schuster

13. *There's No Such Place as Far Away,* by Richard Bach. Delacorte

14. *The Island,* by Peter Benchley. Doubleday

15. *Hanta Yo,* by Ruth Beebe Hill. Doubleday

Nonfiction

1. *Aunt Erma's Cope Book,* by Erma Bombeck. McGraw-Hill

2. *The Complete Scarsdale Medical Diet,* by Herman Tarnower, M. D. and Samm Sinclair Baker. Rawson, Wade

3. *How to Prosper During the Coming Bad Years,* by Howard J. Ruff. Times Books

4. *Cruel Shoes,* by Steve Martin. Putnam

5. *The Pritikin Program for Diet and Exercise,* by Nathan Pritikin and Patrick McGrady Jr. Grosset & Dunlap

6. *White House Years,* by Henry Kissinger. Little, Brown

7. *Lauren Bacall By Myself,* by Lauren Bacall. Knopf

8. *The Brethren: Inside the Supreme Court,* by Bob Woodward and Scott Armstrong. Simon & Schuster

9. *Restoring the American Dream,* by Robert J. Ringer. QED

10. *The Winner's Circle,* by Charles Paul Conn. Revell

11. *The Bronx Zoo,* by Sparky Lyle and Peter Golenbock. Crown

12. *How to Become Financially Independent by Investing in Real Estate,* by Albert J. Lowry. Simon & Schuster

13. *James Herriot's Yorkshire,* by James Herriot. St. Martin's

14. *The Fannie Farmer Cookbook,* by Marion Cunningham. Knopf

15. *The Powers That Be,* by David Halberstam. Knopf

CHAPTER NINE

1980–1989

❧

THE BIG NEWS IN THE 1980s wasn't the books, it was the book business. On the publishing side, a series of mergers and acquisitions began the process that would eventually reduce the number of major book publishers to six big groups, two of them owned by German media companies, one by a British educational and informational publishing conglomerate, and three by American media companies (Viacom, AOL/Time-Warner, and Rupert Murdoch's The News Corporation). In short, the same process that had reduced the role and the number of the small independent bookstores, now took place among publishers, and a long list of hitherto famous American publishing houses either vanished, or were swallowed up to become "imprints" of a larger entity, among them Scribner, Macmillan, Atheneum, Morrow, Putnam, Harper & Row, and Little, Brown.

The ostensible purpose of all this business was to achieve "economy of scale," i.e., spreading the production, warehousing, marketing, and "back-office" costs of a wide range of "imprints" and a larger number of books, and to some extent this was achieved, but at the expense of a certain diversity of taste and tone, which had always distinguished the book publishing business from most others. At the same time, sheer size did not make publishing necessarily more profitable, and most of these big publishing monoliths would continue to disappoint their corporate owners in terms of earnings, except now on a larger scale.

On the bookselling side, the independent stores declined in number to the point where the surviving ones, like the Tattered Cover in Denver, Colorado, or the Madison Avenue Book Shop in New York City, were treated as a national treasures. The Scribner bookstore on Fifth Avenue, perhaps the most beautiful bookstore in the world, became a Benetton store, symbolic, surely, of the trend, while at the level of the "chains," a process similar to that in book publishing promised to reduce the number of major players to two or three, the biggest of which was Barnes & Noble.

The big innovation was the development and strategy of Barnes & Noble's ambitious plans for building "superstores," big bookstores that stood apart from shopping malls, usually offering three or four luxuriously appointed floors, a coffee shop, plenty of parking, and almost every amenity. The superstores would be not just an attempt to build bigger bookstores, but to provide a kind of community center built around books, with "events," visiting authors, a whole program to bring customers into the store, and in many places the superstore became what the library might have been, if the library had money, as well as being bookshops. The superstores would transform bookselling, taking the business of selling books out of the malls and onto the highway, with huge visibility.

One consequence would be that the sales of the top bestselling writers—particularly fiction writers like Tom Clancy, Mary Higgins Clark, Patricia Cornwell, etc.—escalated into seven figures. A million copies in hardcover soon became the benchmark by which "big fiction" was measured, although with a corresponding drop in mass-market sales. People who might have waited for the paperback were being attracted into the big new stores, where discounting made the hardcover not that much more expensive than the paperback (still more was that true at another big phenomenon, the "price clubs," where bestsellers were drastically marked down).

These numbers are in some ways misleading, since nobody has ever been able to figure out how many people read a hardcover book. Judging from my own experience, most hardcover books get passed around to at least three or four people, while mass-market paperbacks don't, in which case a net sale of a million for Mary Higgins Clark probably entails at least 3 or 4 million readers. That's a lot of readers.

This change didn't take place overnight. In 1980, the #1 bestselling novel was James Michener's *The Covenant,* which sold over 500,000 copies— a lot of books, but nothing like what was to come. Taylor Caldwell, who had been on the list since the 1940s, made the list again in 1980, proving that there is a deep, permanent market for successful women's novels, despite the proliferation of books on the list by male writers like Robert Ludlum, Frederick Forsyth, and E. L. Doctorow, while on the nonfiction list there was the usual plethora of books to make the reader wiser, sexier, healthier, or richer: *Crisis Investing, Thy Neighbor's Wife, The Sky's the Limit, Craig Claiborne's Gourmet Diet, Nothing Down, Betty Crocker's International Cookbook, The Coming Currency Collapse,* and *How to Become Financially Independent by Investing in Real Estate.* No less than two of these bestsellers were about investing in real estate, but—speaking as a publisher—I have yet to meet anybody who got rich by buying a book, though quite a lot of people who got rich by writing one. By definition, most financial bestsellers, like most bestselling diet books, represent a fad, a more or less crackpot theory, something, at any rate, that isn't very likely to seem sensible a year later, let alone a decade later. Note, for example, that so far as I know, currency did *not* collapse in the eighties, and while the decade provided plenty of crises (which decade does not?), investing your money to take advantage of them may not be something you can pick up out of a book. The words "Caveat emptor" (Let the buyer beware) are nowhere more important than when perusing the self-help financial, diet, and health shelves in your local bookstore. 1980 also included Shelley Winters's hugely successful autobiography (I published Shelley's less successful sequel to it, thus proving that you should never try to repeat somebody else's success), and Carl Sagan's *Cosmos,* marking the beginning of his hugely successful career as a bestselling popularizer of science.

In 1981 I was the editor for four of the year's bestsellers (not a record— I believe the record is seven, which I think I hold—but still not bad), two of them novels, two nonfiction. The biggest fiction bestseller was James Clavell's *Noble House* (over 500,000) and, in nonfiction, *The Beverly Hills Diet* (nearly 800,000). All Clavell's novels are terrific "reads" (though the best was *King Rat,* the first), but I can't remember what the gimmick of the Beverly Hills diet was, although I think it involved eating a lot of lettuce. Whatever, everybody I knew back then went on it, even women who didn't need to lose weight, and strangely enough most of them were right there to buy the next big diet book when it came along. Diet books represent a state of mind, as much as they do the state of your body—they are, like certain perfume and fashion ads, designed to create fantasy, as much as to show you how to lose weight. If I buy this book, I'll become thin, beautiful, and desirable, is the thought that gets people into the stores, and since nobody is ever as thin, beautiful, and desirable as they want to be, not even the top models, there is always a ready market.

Not surprisingly, given this, two of the big books in 1982 were diet books, *The Weight Watchers Food Plan Diet Cookbook* and Richard Simmons's *Never-Say-Diet Cookbook,* which sold more copies than *The G Spot and Other Recent Discoveries about Human Sexuality,* thus proving that people would rather be thin than have multiple orgasms, no surprise to anybody in the book business. Or that perhaps in our society, people can't tell the difference, that being thin is in and of itself an orgasmic experience.

1982 was William Kotzwinkle's year—*E.T.,* riding on the crest of the immensely successful movie, sold nearly 700,000 copies, putting him ahead of Michener, Ludlum, Sidney Sheldon, Judith Krantz, Jean M. Auel, and

Stephen King. This is not the kind of thing that happens very often; it's like an overweight, unknown runner winning the New York City Marathon, and while it's heartwarming, it is also very hard to repeat.

In 1983 the same thing happened to Michener all over again. *Return of the Jedi* was #1, keeping Michener's *Poland* to #2. Once again the fiction list below #1 was dominated by familiar names: Michener, King, Mailer, le Carré, Danielle Steel, Jackie Collins. The nonfiction list was dominated by get-rich-quick schemes in book form, signifying the Age of Reagan, although beauty, health, and exercise also appeared to be on people's minds. But that figures—we were going to be in for eight years during which making a lot of money and looking good were the predominant national obsessions, and which the successful business books were aimed at top executives, rather than giving their underlings ways in which to rise to the top. It was going to be eight years of good times for those at the top, and this would be reflected in the nonfiction bestsellers of the period.

1984 would show the same tendency to listen to CEOs as if they were the font of wisdom, when Lee Iacocca's autobiography sold over a million copies, followed by a slew of self-confident business books, including *What They Don't Teach You at Harvard Business School: Notes from a Street-Smart Executive*; *Putting the One Minute Manager to Work*; and *Tough Times Never Last, but Tough People Do!*, which captured the zeitgeist of the eighties—at least among white-collar, white upper-middle-income males—perfectly (particularly the last title). *Eat to Win*, at #3, is one of the less appealing diet book titles, but the presence of yet another Weight Watchers book (at #10) indicates the urge to be thin was as compelling as ever. In fiction, once again a familiar list of heavy hitters, with Danielle Steel taking up a yearly place on the list that she still holds eighteen years later.

In 1985, the numbers continued to zoom upward. Jean M. Auel's *The Mammoth Hunters* sold nearly 1,500,000 copies, while Michener's *Texas,* at #2, sold close to 1,400,000 copies—these would have been good mass-market sales a couple of decades earlier. Perhaps for the first time, fiction sales were exceeding nonfiction sales—General Chuck Yeager's autobiography sold over a million copies, while Priscilla Presley's sold 800,000—big numbers, but a lot less than Jean Auel's. No less than three diet books were on the list. In 1986 only two diet books, but six "feel-good" self-help books, showed that the market was still alive and well, while the fiction list once again confirmed that "them that have, gets": King, Clancy, Clavell, Ludlum, Jackie Collins, Danielle Steel, Judith Krantz, Louis L'Amour. There was hardly an unfamiliar name on the list except for Pat Conroy's breakthrough novel *The Prince of Tides.*

At this point, it makes sense to consider another phenomenon of the ripening eighties. As publishers and authors learned that bringing out a book a year by a successful novelist was one of the secrets to higher sales—among other things the publicity for the new book would coincide with the publicity for the mass-market edition of last year's bestseller, thus giving the publisher a double bang for the buck—the number of open "slots" on the bestseller list correspondingly decreased. Even increasing the list from ten books to fifteen didn't solve the problem. If, every year, you had novels by Jean Auel, Danielle Steel, Mary Higgins Clark, Robert Ludlum, James Michener, Sidney Sheldon, John Jakes, Stephen King, and Tom Clancy, that was nine "slots" that wouldn't be available to a newcomer (ten, in fact, since King sometimes had two bestsellers in one year, as would, eventually, and from time to time, Mary Higgins Clark and Danielle Steel). If you add to that bestselling novelists who published a book every two years or eighteen months, like Clive

Cussler or Lawrence Sanders, breaking onto the bestseller list started to become like finding an empty seat on a commuter train that's packed with "regulars," people who commute every day. Huge sales were now necessary to get on the list—certainly to get high on it—and getting to #1 involved prodigies of planning, since the only way to do it was to pick a month when Mary Higgins Clark or Danielle Steel or Stephen King *weren't* publishing a book. In any case, the more successful authors began to appropriate a given date as their own—Mary Higgins Clark's novels, for example, were always published on Mother's Day, while "male adventure/thriller" writers, like Clancy or Cussler, were usually published on Father's Day—the bestseller list began to resemble a club that was hard to break into.

In 1987, for example, out of fifteen novels on the list, only two of them were by somebody who didn't appear on it regularly, Tom Wolfe and Scott Turow, and Wolfe had already been a nonfiction bestseller. It was the nonfiction list on which publishers gambled with new and untried writers—for the fiction list, they tended to compete against each other by trying to buy one or the other of the big-name fiction writers away from their present publisher, for ever-increasing sums of money. For 1988, only *one* of the fifteen novels on the list was by a newcomer and unknown. As for the nonfiction list it was becoming increasingly celebrity driven: Elizabeth Taylor, George Burns, Michael Jackson, Lee Iacocca, Donald Trump. This pattern continued in 1989—again only two books on the fiction list that are not by people who appear on the bestseller list regularly, while the nonfiction list includes Roseanne Barr, Nancy Reagan, Gilda Radner, and a tell-all biography of Jackie Onassis.

On the other hand, at least the *non*fiction list included some challenging and provocative books: Stephen W. Hawking's *A Brief History of Time* and Julia Child's classic *The Way to Cook*. There is no way to avoid concluding from the bestseller lists of the 1980s that American sought safety in buying fiction, by turning to "brand-name" authors, and were more venturesome in buying nonfiction and certainly more receptive to new, challenging, or difficult ideas, as with Hawking's book.

Once again, the top fiction titles sold in enormous numbers—upward of 1,600,000 copies, for Clancy, for example, and for King. With numbers like these the large corporations, which now owned the lion's share of book publishing, must have wondered why publishing wasn't more profitable. Way back in the 1950s, Leon Shimkin, the cofounder of Pocket Books and then co-owner of Simon & Schuster, had commissioned an exhaustive statistical study of which books made money. It was presented to us at a long meeting, and the man in charge of the project ended his presentation by staring at the editors and saying, "Do you guys realize how much money the company would make if you only published bestsellers?"

By the 1980s there were plenty of corporate voices asking that same question again. The answer—that you wouldn't have the bestsellers without publishing new and talented writers—wasn't accepted with any better grace thirty years later, but remained just as true.

1980

FICTION

1. *The Covenant,* by James A. Michener. Random House

2. *The Bourne Identity,* by Robert Ludlum. Richard Marek

3. *Rage of Angels,* by Sidney Sheldon. Morrow

4. *Princess Daisy,* by Judith Krantz. Crown

5. *Firestarter,* by Stephen King. Viking

6. *The Key to Rebecca,* by Ken Follett. Morrow

7. *Random Winds,* by Belva Plain. Delacorte

8. *The Devil's Alternative,* by Frederick Forsyth. Viking

9. *The Fifth Horseman,* by Larry Collins and Dominique Lapierre. Simon & Schuster

10. *The Spike,* by Arnaud de Borchgrave and Robert Moss. Crown

11. *Come Pour the Wine,* by Cynthia Freeman. Arbor House

12. *Fanny, Being the True History of the Adventures of Fanny Hackabout Jones,* by Erica Jong. NAL Books

13. *Loon Lake,* by E. L. Doctorow. Random House

14. *Answer as a Man,* by Taylor Caldwell. Putnam

15. *The Tenth Commandment,* by Lawrence Sanders. Putnam

NONFICTION

1. *Crisis Investing: Opportunities and Profits in the Coming Great Depression,* by Douglas R. Casey. Stratford Press

2. *Cosmos,* by Carl Sagan. Random House

3. *Free to Choose: A Personal Statement,* by Milton and Rose Friedman. Harcourt Brace Jovanovich

4. *Anatomy of an Illness as Perceived by the Patient,* by Norman Cousins. Norton

5. *Thy Neighbor's Wife,* by Gay Talese. Doubleday

6. *The Sky's the Limit,* by Dr. Wayne W. Dyer. Simon & Schuster

7. *The Third Wave,* by Alvin Toffler. Morrow

8. *Craig Claiborne's Gourmet Diet,* by Craig Claiborne with Pierre Franey. Times Books

9. *Nothing Down,* by Robert Allen. Simon & Schuster

10. *Shelley Also Known as Shirley,* by Shelley Winters. Morrow

11. *Side Effects,* by Woody Allen. Random House

12. *Jim Fixx's Second Book of Running,* by James F. Fixx. Random House

13. *Betty Crocker's International Cookbook,* Random House

14. *The Coming Currency Collapse and What to Do about It,* by Jerome F. Smith. Books in Focus

15. *How to Become Financially Independent by Investing in Real Estate,* by Albert J. Lowry. Simon & Schuster

1981

FICTION

1. *Noble House*, by James Clavell. Delacorte

2. *The Hotel New Hampshire*, by John Irving. A Henry Robbins Book/Dutton

3. *Cujo*, by Stephen King. Viking

4. *An Indecent Obsession*, by Colleen McCullough. Harper & Row

5. *Gorky Park*, by Martin Cruz Smith. Random House

6. *Masquerade*, by Kit Williams. Schocken Books

7. *Goodbye, Janette*, by Harold Robbins. Simon & Schuster

8. *The Third Deadly Sin*, by Lawrence Sanders. Putnam

9. *The Glitter Dome*, by Joseph Wambaugh. Perigord Press/Morrow

10. *No Time for Tears*, by Cynthia Freeman. Arbor House

11. *God Emperor of Dune*, by Frank Herbert. Putnam

12. *The Legacy*, by Howard Fast. Houghton Mifflin

13. *The Cardinal Sins*, by Andrew M. Greeley. Warner/Bernard Geis

14. *The Last Days of America*, by Paul Erdman. Simon & Schuster

15. *Free Fall in Crimson*, by John D. MacDonald. Harper & Row

NONFICTION

1. *The Beverly Hills Diet,* by Judy Mazel. Macmillan

2. *The Lord God Made Them All,* by James Herriot. St. Martin's

3. *Richard Simmons' Never-Say-Diet Book,* by Richard Simmons. Warner

4. *A Light in the Attic,* by Shel Silverstein. Harper & Row

5. *Cosmos,* by Carl Sagan. Random House

6. *Better Homes and Gardens New Cookbook.* Meredith

7. *Miss Piggy's Guide to Life,* by Miss Piggy as told to Henry Beard. Knopf

8. *Weight Watchers® 365-Day Menu Cookbook.* NAL Books

9. *You Can Negotiate Anything,* by Herb Cohen. Lyle Stuart

10. *A Few Minutes with Andy Rooney,* by Andrew A. Rooney. Atheneum

11. *Pathfinders,* by Gail Sheehy. Morrow

12. *How to Make Love to a Man,* by Alexandra Penney. Clarkson N. Potter

13. *The Walk West,* by Peter and Barbara Jenkins. Morrow

14. *Elizabeth Taylor: The Last Star,* by Kitty Kelley. Simon & Schuster

15. *The Eagle's Gift,* by Carlos Castaneda. Simon & Schuster

1982

FICTION

1. *E. T. The Extra-Terrestrial Storybook,* by William Kotzwinkle. Putnam

2. *Space,* by James A. Michener. Random House

3. *The Parsifal Mosaic,* by Robert Ludlum. Random House

4. *Master of the Game,* by Sidney Sheldon. Morrow

5. *Mistral's Daughter,* by Judith Krantz. Crown

6. *The Valley of Horses,* by Jean M. Auel. Crown

7. *Different Seasons,* by Stephen King. Viking

8. *North and South,* by John Jakes. Harcourt Brace Jovanovich

9. *2010: Odyssey Two,* by Arthur C. Clarke. A Del Rey Book/Ballantine

10. *The Man from St. Petersburg,* by Ken Follett. Morrow

11. *The Prodigal Daughter,* by Jeffrey Archer. Linden Press

12. *Foundation's Edge,* by Isaac Asimov. Doubleday

13. *Crossings,* by Danielle Steel. Delacorte

14. *The One Tree: Book Two of The Second Chronicles of Thomas Covenant,* by Stephen R. Donaldson. A Del Rey Book/Ballantine

15. *Spellbinder,* by Harold Robbins. Simon & Schuster

NONFICTION

1. *Jane Fonda's Workout Book,* by Jane Fonda. Simon & Schuster

2. *Living, Loving and Learning,* by Leo Buscaglia. Charles B. Slack/Holt, Rinehart & Winston

3. *And More by Andy Rooney,* by Andrew A. Rooney. Atheneum

4. *Better Homes and Gardens New Cookbook.* Meredith

5. *Life Extension: Adding Years to Your Life and Life to Your Years—A Practical Scientific Approach,* by Durk Pearson and Sandy Shaw. Warner

6. *When Bad Things Happen to Good People,* by Harold S. Kushner. Schocken

7. *A Few Minutes with Andy Rooney,* by Andrew A. Rooney. Atheneum

8. *The Weight Watchers® Food Plan Diet Cookbook,* by Jean Nidetch. NAL Books

9. *Richard Simmons' Never-Say-Diet Cookbook,* by Richard Simmons. Warner

10. *No Bad Dogs: The Woodhouse Way,* by Barbara Woodhouse. Summit Books

11. *Weight Watchers® 365-Day Menu Cookbook,* by Weight Watchers International. NAL Books

12. *The Fall of Freddie the Leaf,* by Leo Buscaglia. Charles B. Slack/Holt, Rinehart and Winston

13. *The G Spot and Other Recent Discoveries about Human Sexuality,* by Alice Kahn Ladas, Beverly Whipple, and John D. Perry. Holt, Rinehart & Winston

14. *An Uncommon Freedom,* by Charles Paul Conn. Revell

15. *Megatrends: Ten New Directions Transforming Our Lives,* by John Naisbitt. Warner

1983

FICTION

1. *Return of the Jedi™ Storybook,* adapted by Joan D. Vinge. Random House

2. *Poland,* by James A. Michener. Random House

3. *Pet Sematary,* by Stephen King. Doubleday

4. *The Little Drummer Girl,* by John le Carré. Knopf

5. *Christine,* by Stephen King. Viking

6. *Changes,* by Danielle Steel. Delacorte

7. *The Name of the Rose,* by Umberto Eco. A Helen and Kurt Wolff Book/ Harcourt Brace Jovanovich

8. *White Gold Wielder: Book Three of The Second Chronicles of Thomas Covenant,* by Stephen R. Donaldson. Del Rey/Ballantine

9. *Hollywood Wives,* by Jackie Collins. Simon & Schuster

10. *The Lonesome Gods,* by Louis L'Amour. Bantam

11. *Who Killed the Robins Family?* by Bill Adler and Thomas Chastain. Morrow

12. *The Robots of Dawn,* by Isaac Asimov. Doubleday

13. *August,* by Judith Rossner. Houghton Mifflin

14. *Ancient Evenings,* by Norman Mailer. Little, Brown

15. *Moreta: Dragonlady of Pern,* by Anne McCaffrey. Del Rey/Ballantine

Nonfiction

1. *In Search of Excellence: Lessons from America's Best-Run Companies,* by Thomas J. Peters and Robert H. Waterman Jr. Harper & Row

2. *Megatrends: Ten New Directions Transforming Our Lives,* by John Naisbitt. Warner

3. *Motherhood: The Second Oldest Profession,* by Erma Bombeck. McGraw-Hill

4. *The One Minute Manager,* by Kenneth Blanchard and Spencer Johnson. Morrow

5. *Jane Fonda's Workout Book,* by Jane Fonda. Simon & Schuster

6. *The Best of James Herriot,* by James Herriot. St. Martin's

7. *The Mary Kay Guide to Beauty: Discovering Your Special Look,* by the Beauty Experts at Mary Kay Cosmetics. Addison-Wesley

8. *On Wings of Eagles,* by Ken Follett. Morrow

9. *Creating Wealth,* by Robert G. Allen. Simon & Schuster

10. *The Body Principal: The Exercise Program for Life,* by Victoria Principal. Simon & Schuster

11. *Approaching Hoofbeats: The Four Horsemen of the Apocalypse,* by Billy Graham. Word

12. *Tough Times Never Last, but Tough People Do!,* by Robert H. Schuller. Thomas Nelson

13. *Blue Highways: A Journey into America,* by William Least Heat Moon. Atlantic Monthly Press/Little, Brown

14. *The Secret Kingdom,* by Pat Robertson with Bob Slosser. Thoman Nelson

15. *While Reagan Slept,* by Art Buchwald. Putnam

1984

FICTION

1. *The Talisman,* by Stephen King and Peter Straub. Viking

2. *The Aquitaine Progression,* by Robert Ludlum. Random House

3. *The Sicilian,* by Mario Puzo. Linden Press/Simon & Schuster

4. *Love and War,* by John Jakes. Harcourt Brace Jovanovich

5. *The Butter Battle Book,* by Dr. Seuss. Random House

6. *"…And Ladies of the Club,"* by Helen Hooven Santmyer. Putnam

7. *The Fourth Protocol,* by Frederick Forsyth. Viking

8. *Full Circle,* by Danielle Steel. Delacorte

9. *The Life and Hard Times of Heidi Abromowitz,* by Joan Rivers. Delacorte

10. *Lincoln: A Novel,* by Gore Vidal. Random House

11. *The Walking Drum,* by Louis L'Amour. Bantam

12. *The Haj,* by Leon Uris. Doubleday

13. *Strong Medicine,* by Arthur Hailey. Doubleday

14. *First Among Equals,* by Jeffrey Archer. Linden Press/Simon & Schuster

15. *The Dune Storybook,* adapted by Joan D. Vinge. Putnam

NONFICTION

1. *Iacocca: An Autobiography,* by Lee Iacocca with William Novak. Bantam Books

2. *Loving Each Other,* by Leo Buscaglia. Slack/Holt, Rinehart & Winston

3. *Eat to Win: The Sports Nutrition Bible,* by Robert Haas, M. D. Rawson Associates

4. *Pieces of My Mind,* by Andrew A. Rooney. Atheneum

5. *Weight Watchers® Fast and Fabulous Cookbook,* by Weight Watchers International. NAL Books

6. *What They Don't Teach You at Harvard Business School: Notes from a Street-Smart Executive,* by Mark H. McCormack. Bantam Books

7. *Women Coming of Age,* by Jane Fonda with Mignon McCarthy. Simon & Schuster

8. *Moses the Kitten,* by James Herriot. St. Martin's

9. *The One Minute Salesperson,* by Spencer Johnson, M. D. and Larry Wilson. Morrow

10. *Weight Watchers® Quick Start® Program Cookbook,* by Jean Nidetch. NAL Books

11. *Chef Paul Prudhomme's Louisiana Kitchen,* by Paul Prudhomme. Morrow

12. *Putting the One Minute Manager to Work,* by Kenneth Blanchard and Robert Lorber. Morrow

13. *Tough Times Never Last, but Tough People Do!,* by Robert H. Schuller. Thomas Nelson

14. *The Bridge Across Forever,* by Richard Bach. Morrow

15. *Dr. Burns' Prescription for Happiness,* by George Burns. Putnam

1985

FICTION

1. *The Mammoth Hunters,* by Jean M. Auel. Crown

2. *Texas,* by James A. Michener. Random House

3. *Lake Wobegon Days,* by Garrison Keillor. Viking

4. *If Tomorrow Comes,* by Sidney Sheldon. Morrow

5. *Skeleton Crew,* by Stephen King. Putnam

6. *Secrets,* by Danielle Steel. Delacorte Press

7. *Contact,* by Carl Sagan. Simon & Schuster

8. *Lucky,* by Jackie Collins. Simon & Schuster

9. *Family Album,* by Danielle Steel. Delacorte

10. *Jubal Sackett,* by Louis L'Amour. Bantam Books

11. *Thinner,* by Stephen King, writing as Richard Bachman. NAL Books

12. *Cider House Rules,* by John Irving. Morrow

13. *The Hunt for Red October,* by Tom Clancy. Naval Institute Press

14. *The Fourth Deadly Sin,* by Lawrence Sanders. Putnam

15. *Inside, Outside,* by Herman Wouk. Little, Brown

NONFICTION

1. *Iacocca: An Autobiography,* by Lee Iacocca with William Novak.
    Bantam Books

2. *Yeager: An Autobiography,* by General Chuck Yeager and Leo Janos.
    Bantam Books

3. *Elvis and Me,* by Priscilla Beaulieu Presley with Sandra Harmon. Putnam

4. *Fit for Life,* by Harvey and Marilyn Diamond. Warner Books

5. *The Be-Happy Attitudes,* by Robert Schuller. Word

6. *Dancing in the Light,* by Shirley MacLaine. Bantam Books

7. *A Passion for Excellence: The Leadership Difference,* by Thomas J. Peters
    and Nancy K. Austin. Random House

8. *The Frugal Gourmet,* by Jeff Smith. Morrow

9. *I Never Played the Game,* by Howard Cosell with Peter Bonventre. Morrow

10. *Dr. Berger's Immune Power Diet,* by Stuart M. Berger, M. D. NAL Books

11. *Weight Watchers® Quick Start® Program Cookbook,* by Jean Nidetch.
    NAL Books

12. *Smart Women, Foolish Choices: Finding the Right Men and
    Avoiding the Wrong Ones,* by Dr. Connell Cowan and Dr. Melvyn Kinder.
    Clarkson N. Potter

13. *On the Road with Charles Kuralt,* by Charles Kuralt. Putnam

14. *Weight Watchers® New International Cookbook,* by Jean Nidetch.
    NAL Books

15. *Loving Each Other,* by Leo Buscaglia. Slack/Henry Holt & Co.

1986

FICTION

1. *It,* by Stephen King. Viking

2. *Red Storm Rising,* by Tom Clancy. Putnam

3. *Whirlwind,* by James Clavell. Morrow

4. *The Bourne Supremacy,* by Robert Ludlum. Random House

5. *Hollywood Husbands,* by Jackie Collins. Simon & Schuster

6. *Wanderlust,* by Danielle Steel. Delacorte Press

7. *I'll Take Manhattan,* by Judith Krantz. Crown

8. *Last of the Breed,* by Louis L'Amour. Bantam

9. *The Prince of Tides,* by Pat Conroy. Houghton Mifflin

10. *A Perfect Spy,* by John le Carré. Knopf

11. *A Matter of Honor,* by Jeffrey Archer. Linden Press

12. *Lie Down with Lions,* by Ken Follett. Morrow

13. *The Eighth Commandment,* by Lawrence Sanders. Putnam

14. *Act of Will,* by Barbara Taylor Bradford. Doubleday

15. *Cyclops,* by Clive Cussler. Simon & Schuster

NONFICTION

1. *Fatherhood,* by Bill Cosby. Doubleday

2. *Fit for Life,* by Harvey and Marilyn Diamond. Warner Books

3. *His Way: The Unauthorized Biography of Frank Sinatra,* by Kitty Kelley. Bantam

4. *The Rotation Diet,* by Martin Katahn. Norton

5. *You're Only Old Once,* by Dr. Seuss. Random House

6. *Callanetics: Ten Years Younger in Ten Hours,* by Callan Pinckney. Morrow

7. *The Frugal Gourmet Cooks with Wine,* by Jeff Smith. Morrow

8. *Be Happy—You Are Loved!* by Robert H. Schuller. Thomas Nelson

9. *Word for Word,* by Andrew A. Rooney. Putnam

10. *James Herriot's Dog Stories,* by James Herriot. St. Martin's

11. *McMahon!: The Bare Truth About Chicago's Brashest Bear,* by Jim McMahon with Bob Verdi. Warner Books

12. *The Frugal Gourmet,* by Jeff Smith. Morrow

13. *Men Who Hate Women and the Women Who Love Them,* by Dr. Susan Forward and Joan Torres. Bantam

14. *One More Time,* by Carol Burnett. Random House

15. *Bus 9 to Paradise,* by Leo Buscaglia. Morrow/Slack

1987

FICTION

1. *The Tommyknockers,* by Stephen King. Putnam

2. *Patriot Games,* by Tom Clancy. Putnam

3. *Kaleidoscope,* by Danielle Steel. Delacorte Press

4. *Misery,* by Stephen King. Viking

5. *Leaving Home: A Collection of Lake Wobegon Stories,* by Garrison Keillor. Viking

6. *Windmills of the Gods,* by Sidney Sheldon. Morrow

7. *Presumed Innocent,* by Scott Turow. Farrar, Straus & Giroux

8. *Fine Things,* by Danielle Steel. Delacorte Press

9. *Heaven and Hell,* by John Jakes. Harcourt Brace Jovanovich

10. *The Eyes of the Dragon,* by Stephen King. Viking

11. *The Haunted Mesa,* by Louis L'Amour. Bantam

12. *The Bonfire of the Vanities,* by Tom Wolfe. Farrar, Straus & Giroux

13. *Legacy,* by James A. Michener. Random House

14. *2061: Odyssey Three,* by Arthur C. Clarke. Del Rey/Ballantine

15. *Weep No More My Lady,* by Mary Higgins Clark. Simon & Schuster

Nonfiction

1. *Time Flies,* by Bill Cosby. Doubleday/Dolphin

2. *Spycatcher: The Candid Autobiography of a Senior Intelligence Officer,* by Peter Wright with Paul Greengrass. Viking

3. *Family: The Ties That Bind...and Gag!* by Erma Bombeck. McGraw-Hill

4. *Veil: The Secret Wars of the CIA, 1981–1987,* by Bob Woodward. Simon & Schuster

5. *A Day in the Life of America,* by Rick Smolan and David Cohen. Collins Publishers

6. *The Great Depression of 1990,* by Ravi Batra. Simon & Schuster

7. *It's All in the Playing,* by Shirley MacLaine. Bantam

8. *Man of the House: The Life and Political Memoirs of Speaker Tip O'Neill,* by Thomas P. O'Neill Jr. with William Novak. Random House

9. *The Frugal Gourmet Cooks American,* by Jeff Smith. Morrow

10. *The Closing of the American Mind,* by Allan Bloom. Simon & Schuster

11. *Free to Be...a Family,* by Marlo Thomas and Friends. Bantam

12. *A Day in the Life of the Soviet Union,* by Rick Smolan & David Cohen. Collins Publishers

13. *Love, Medicine & Miracles,* by Bernie S. Siegel. Harper & Row

14. *A Season on the Brink,* by John Feinstein. Macmillan

15. *Thriving on Chaos: Handbook for a Management Revolution,* by Tom Peters. Knopf

1988

FICTION

1. *The Cardinal of the Kremlin,* by Tom Clancy. Putnam

2. *The Sands of Time,* by Sidney Sheldon. Morrow

3. *Zoya,* by Danielle Steel. Delacorte Press

4. *The Icarus Agenda,* by Robert Ludlum. Random House

5. *Alaska,* by James A. Michener. Random House

6. *Till We Meet Again,* by Judith Krantz. Crown

7. *The Queen of the Damned,* by Anne Rice. Knopf

8. *To Be the Best,* by Barbara Taylor Bradford. Doubleday

9. *One: A Novel,* by Richard Bach. Morrow/Silver Arrow Books

10. *Mitla Pass,* by Leon Uris. Doubleday

11. *The Bonfire of the Vanities,* by Tom Wolfe. Farrar, Straus & Giroux

12. *Final Flight,* by Stephen Coonts. Doubleday

13. *Rock Star,* by Jackie Collins. Simon & Schuster

14. *Dear Mili,* by Wilhelm Grimm with illustrations by Maurice Sendak. Farrar, Straus & Giroux/Michael di Capua Books

15. *Hot Money,* by Dick Francis. Putnam

NONFICTION

1. *The 8-Week Cholesterol Cure,* by Robert E. Kowalski. Harper & Row

2. *Talking Straight,* by Lee Iacocca with Sonny Kleinfield. Bantam

3. *A Brief History of Time: From the Big Bang to Black Holes,* by Stephen W. Hawking. Bantam

4. *Trump: The Art of the Deal,* by Donald J. Trump with Tony Schwartz. Random House

5. *Gracie: A Love Story,* by George Burns. Putnam

6. *Elizabeth Takes Off,* by Elizabeth Taylor. Putnam

7. *Swim with the Sharks without Being Eaten Alive,* by Harvey MacKay. Morrow

8. *Christmas in America,* ed. by David Cohen. Collins Publishers

9. *Weight Watchers® Quick Success Program Cookbook,* by Jean Nidetch. NAL Books

10. *Moonwalk,* by Michael Jackson. Doubleday

11. *All I Really Need to Know I Learned in Kindergarten: Uncommon Thoughts on Common Things,* by Robert Fulghum. Villard Books

12. *For the Record: From Wall Street to Washington,* by Donald T. Regan. Harcourt Brace Jovanovich

13. *The Sackett Companion: A Personal Guide to the Sackett Novels,* by Louis L'Amour. Bantam

14. *Weight Watchers® Quick and Easy Menu Cookbook,* by Weight Watchers International. NAL Books

15. *Seven Stories of Christmas Love,* by Leo Buscaglia. Morrow/Slack

1989

FICTION

1. *Clear and Present Danger,* by Tom Clancy. Putnam

2. *The Dark Half,* by Stephen King. Viking

3. *Daddy,* by Danielle Steel. Delacorte Press

4. *Star,* by Danielle Steel. Delacorte Press

5. *Caribbean,* by James A. Michener. Random House

6. *The Satanic Verses,* by Salman Rushdie. Viking

7. *The Russia House,* by John le Carré. Knopf

8. *The Pillars of the Earth,* by Ken Follett. Morrow

9. *California Gold,* by John Jakes. Random House

10. *While My Pretty One Sleeps,* by Mary Higgins Clark. Simon & Schuster

11. *Midnight,* by Dean R. Koontz. Putnam

12. *Jimmy Stewart and His Poems,* by Jimmy Stewart. Crown

13. *The Negotiator,* by Frederick Forsyth. Bantam Books

14. *Straight,* by Dick Francis. Putnam

15. *Polar Star,* by Martin Cruz Smith. Random House

NONFICTION

1. *All I Really Need to Know I Learned in Kindergarten: Uncommon Thoughts on Common Things,* by Robert Fulghum. Villard Books

2. *Wealth Without Risk: How to Develop a Personal Fortune Without Going Out on a Limb,* by Charles J. Givens. Simon & Schuster

3. *A Woman Named Jackie,* by C. David Heymann. Lyle Stuart Book/Carol Publishing Group

4. *It Was on Fire When I Lay Down on It,* by Robert Fulghum. Villard Books

5. *Better Homes and Gardens New Cook Book.* Better Homes and Gardens Books

6. *The Way Things Work,* by David Macaulay. Houghton Mifflin

7. *It's Always Something,* by Gilda Radner. Simon & Schuster

8. *Roseanne: My Life as a Woman,* by Roseanne Barr. Harper & Row

9. *The Frugal Gourmet Cooks Three Ancient Cuisines: China, Greece, and Rome,* by Jeff Smith. Morrow

10. *My Turn: The Memoirs of Nancy Reagan,* by Nancy Reagan with William Novak. Random House

11. *All My Best Friends,* by George Burns written with David Fisher. Putnam

12. *Love & Marriage,* by Bill Cosby. Doubleday

13. *A Brief History of Time,* by Stephen W. Hawking. Bantam

14. *Blind Faith,* by Joe McGinniss. Putnam

15. *The Way to Cook,* by Julia Child. Knopf

CHAPTER TEN

1990–1999

એર

T HE RICH GET RICHER, and the poor get poorer," might have been the theme for the early nineties, both in terms of the increasing consolidation of the book industry, at both ends, bookselling and book publishing, and the predictability of the bestseller list. In 1990, for example, the fiction list for the year contained not a single newcomer—all fifteen who made it were established, familiar bestselling writers, most of them on a yearly basis. It was, if you like, the triumph of brand-name merchandizing applied to books. Even the nonfiction consisted mostly of celebrities (Ronald Reagan, Charles Kuralt, Bo Jackson, Barbara Mandrell, Barbara Bush, Cleveland Amory), or self-help books *(Financial Self-Defense, Wealth Without Risk)*, or history based on an enormously successful PBS series *(The Civil War)*, or cookbooks *(The Frugal Gourmet* and *Better Homes and Gardens New Cook Book)*. This is the period when publishers were playing it safe—no surprises, not much in the way of new talent, a pronounced preference for the old, the familiar, and the proven.

1991 was a little better, though the #1 bestselling novel was Alexandra Ripley's *Scarlett*, a sequel to *Gone With the Wind*, which sold nearly 2,200,000 copies between September 25th and the end of the year, according to *PW*, and therefore the fastest-selling novel in history, as well as, in retrospect, one of the most quickly forgotten. 1991 introduced John Grisham to the ranks of the million-copy-plus once-a-year repeaters, but otherwise it was a fairly predictable list. The indomitable Katharine Hepburn topped the nonfiction list at #1, followed by a mix of self-help books and star journalists' histories of recent events: James B. Stewart on the Wall Street scandals, Bob Woodward on the war with Iraq, Kitty Kelley on Nancy Reagan's life and times, while Colonel Oliver North told his own story.

1992 brought about much the same results: a fiction list consisting almost entirely of regularly appearing megastars (King twice, Grisham,

Danielle Steel twice, Sidney Sheldon, Anne Rice, James Michener, Mary Higgins Clark, Clive Cussler, Dean R. Koontz, Robert Ludlum, Judith Krantz), though a somewhat more varied nonfiction list.

This was a bad time for beginners, frankly, particularly novelists. You looked at the list and practically every slot was taken up by a familiar name; you looked at the bookshops, and all you saw displayed up front were writers who sold a million copies or more; you called your agent and discovered that he or she was only taking calls from writers who hit the list on their publication day, did at least one book a year, and sold to the movies or television for megabucks. It was not even that good a time for publishers. Gambling on the new, the untried, the original is the life blood of publishing, and a publishing house that plays it safe, even if it satisfies its corporate parent, will sooner or later collapse.

The nonfiction list at least offered a little more hope. It was still dominated by celebrities—Rush Limbaugh, General Norman Schwarzkopf, Sam Walton, Madonna, Kathie Lee Gifford, a biography of Princess Diana—but David McCullough's monumental biography of Truman proved that people would still read serious history and biography if it were offered to them; here, at least, was a real book on the list.

A small ray of hope appeared on the list in 1993—Laura Esquivel's *Like Water for Chocolate* and James Waller's *The Bridges of Madison County.* Neither of these is exactly Proust, but here, at least, were two new and previously unknown novelists on a list that otherwise seems totally familiar: Grisham, Clancy, King, Steel, Clark, Clavell, Koontz, Follett, Ludlum, etc. Nonfiction was again dominated by celebrities, and included two books by Rush Limbaugh, one by Howard Stern, and one by Jerry Seinfeld. As usual, a lot of self-help books, but it is interesting to note that the nineties was beginning to feature a different kind of self-help book, signaling, as self-help books always do, a major shift in the way people lived.

First of all, as opposed to the get-rich, get-thin bestsellers of the previous decade, the trend was toward spiritual enlightenment—*Ageless Body, Timeless Mind* by Deepak Chopra being typical—and good health through sensible nutrition—viz., Susan Powter's *Stop the Insanity.* At the same time, books that set out to explain how women relate to the universe (and to men) leapt onto the list, among them *Women Who Run with the Wolves* and *Men Are from Mars, Women Are from Venus.* Increasingly, the self-help market would be divided into books written for women and books written for men, while the focus would be less in making people richer or more successful, or even happier, than in trying to find or invent a kind of spiritual/anthropological basis for human behavior, a Darwinian solution for those who felt themselves to be searching for an identity, and hoped to find the answer in animals, or primitive tribes, or in the genetic programming of the genders.

1994 was more of the same—the usual suspects on the fiction list and a nonfiction list of celebrities, ranging from the Pope to Dolly Parton and Barbara Bush. Even the cookbooks were celebrity driven, including *The Bubba Gump Shrimp Co. Cookbook,* based on the success of the movie *Forrest Gump,* and *In the Kitchen with Rosie* (which sold almost 6 million copies). Three of the nonfiction slots were taken by 3-D illustrated books, pure "merchandise." A large proportion of the 1995 list consisted of repeats from the 1994 list—the big bestsellers were becoming so big, like *In the Kitchen with Rosie* and *Men Are from Mars, Women Are from Venus,* that they stayed on the list for a couple of years, selling on and on. Numbers, too, escalated, with the concentrated merchandizing of the superstores and the price clubs. On the fiction list, for example, each of the first three novels sold over 1,500,000 copies—Grisham, at #1, reached almost 2,400,000 in hardcover, and in 1996 reached #1 again, with sales of nearly 2,800,000! This pattern would hold in 1997, except for the fact that, thank God, the #2 bestselling novel (after Grisham's *The Partner,* at 2,600,000 copies) was Charles Frazier's *Cold Mountain,* a brilliant, original, and literary first novel set in the Civil War, and which all by itself restored the book industry's ebbing faith that a first novel—let alone a *good* first novel—could make it into the upper ranks of the bestseller list. I cracked open a splendid bottle of wine to celebrate Frazier's success, even though I was not, regrettably, his publisher. In Voltaire's famous phrase about God, *"Si Dieu n'existait pas, il faudrait l'inventer."*

The 1997 nonfiction list contained the stupendously successful *Midnight in the Garden of Good and Evil,* proof again that Americans would read a good book if somebody took the trouble to sell one to them, as well as Jon Krakauer's *Into Thin Air,* one of the great adventure books. Through 1998 and 1999, the same held true: predictable fiction bestsellers, netting, at the top, enormous numbers, with the nonfiction list dominated by big names like Peter Jennings and Tom Brokaw, and self-help books whose titles sound like greeting cards (*Don't Sweat the Small Stuff in Love*).

At the end of the day, the bestseller lists of the nineties made for relatively depressing reading, except to accountants. In fiction, it became enormously difficult to break through the sheer weight of numbers generated by perhaps two dozen, or fewer, top writers, who virtually dominated the list, and in nonfiction, a range of celebrities, merchandise, and self-help books that made it equally hard for all but the most exceptional book to get on the list.

1990

FICTION

1. *The Plains of Passage,* by Jean M. Auel. Crown

2. *Four Past Midnight,* by Stephen King. Viking

3. *The Burden of Proof,* by Scott Turow. Farrar, Straus & Giroux

4. *Memories of Midnight,* by Sidney Sheldon. Morrow

5. *Message from Nam,* by Danielle Steel. Delacorte

6. *The Bourne Ultimatum,* by Robert Ludlum. Random House

7. *The Stand: The Complete & Uncut Edition,* by Stephen King. Doubleday

8. *Lady Boss,* by Jackie Collins. Simon & Schuster

9. *The Witching Hour,* by Anne Rice. Knopf

10. *September,* by Rosamunde Pilcher. St. Martin's/A Thomas Dunne Book

11. *Dazzle,* by Judith Krantz. Crown

12. *The Bad Place,* by Dean R. Koontz. Putnam

13. *The Women in His Life,* by Barbara Taylor Bradford. Random House

14. *The First Man in Rome,* by Colleen McCullough. Morrow

15. *Dragon,* by Clive Cussler. Simon & Schuster

Nonfiction

1. *A Life on the Road,* by Charles Kuralt. Putnam

2. *The Civil War,* by Geoffrey C. Ward with Ric Burns and Ken Burns. Knopf

3. *The Frugal Gourmet on Our Immigrant Heritage: Recipes You Should Have Gotten from Your Grandmother,* by Jeff Smith. Morrow

4. *Better Homes and Gardens New Cook Book,* by Better Homes and Gardens Editors. Better Homes and Gardens

5. *Financial Self-Defense: How to Win the Fight for Financial Freedom,* by Charles J. Givens. Simon & Schuster

6. *Homecoming: Reclaiming and Championing Your Inner Child,* by John Bradshaw. Bantam

7. *Wealth Without Risk: How to Develop a Personal Fortune Without Going Out on a Limb,* by Charles J. Givens. Simon & Schuster

8. *Bo Knows Bo,* by Bo Jackson and Dick Schaap. Doubleday

9. *An American Life: An Autobiography,* by Ronald Reagan. Simon & Schuster

10. *Megatrends 2000: Ten New Directions for the 1990s,* by John Naisbett and Patricia Aburdene. Morrow

11. *By Way of Deception: The Making and Unmaking of a Mossad Officer,* by Victor Ostrovsky and Claire Hoy. St. Martin's

12. *Get to the Heart: My Story,* by Barbara Mandrell and George Vecsey. Bantam

13. *Millie's Book: As Dictated to Barbara Bush,* by Mildred Kerr Bush. Morrow

14. *Men At Work: The Craft of Baseball,* by George F. Will. Macmillan

15. *The Cat and the Curmudgeon,* by Cleveland Amory. Little, Brown

1991

FICTION

1. *Scarlett: The Sequel to Margaret Mitchell's* Gone With the Wind, by Alexandra Ripley. Warner Books

2. *The Sum of All Fears,* by Tom Clancy. Putnam

3. *Needful Things,* by Stephen King. Viking Penquin

4. *No Greater Love,* by Danielle Steel. Delacorte

5. *Heartbeat,* by Danielle Steel. Delacorte

6. *The Doomsday Conspiracy,* by Sidney Sheldon. Morrow

7. *The Firm,* by John Grisham. Doubleday

8. *Night Over Water,* by Ken Follett. Morrow

9. *Remember,* by Barbara Taylor Bradford. Random House

10. *Loves Music, Loves to Dance,* by Mary Higgins Clark. Simon & Schuster

11. *Cold Fire,* by Dean R. Koontz. Putnam

12. *The Kitchen God's Wife,* by Amy Tan. Putnam

13. *Sleeping Beauty,* by Judith Michael. Poseidon Books

14. *Star Wars: Heir to the Empire,* by Timothy Zahn. Bantam

15. *WLT: A Radio Romance,* by Garrison Keillor. Viking

NONFICTION

1. *Me: Stories of My Life,* by Katharine Hepburn. Knopf

2. *Nancy Reagan: The Unauthorized Biography,* by Kitty Kelley. Simon & Schuster

3. *Uh-Oh: Some Observations from Both Sides of the Refrigerator Door,* by Robert Fulghum. Villard Books

4. *Under Fire: An American Story,* by Oliver North with William Novak. HarperCollins

5. *Final Exit: The Practicalities of Self-Deliverance and Assisted Suicide for the Dying,* by Derek Humphry. Hemlock/Carol

6. *When You Look Like Your Passport Photo, It's Time to Go Home,* by Erma Bombeck. HarperCollins

7. *More Wealth Without Risk,* by Charles J. Givens. Simon & Schuster

8. *Den of Thieves,* by James B. Stewart. Simon & Schuster

9. *Childhood,* by Bill Cosby. Putnam

10. *Financial Self-Defense,* by Charles J. Givens. Simon & Schuster

11. *The Frugal Gourmet Celebrates Christmas,* by Jeff Smith. Morrow

12. *Iron John: A Book About Men,* by Robert Bly. Addison-Wesley

13. *The Commanders,* by Bob Woodward. Simon & Schuster

14. *The Best Treatment,* by Isadore Rosenfeld, M. D. Simon & Schuster

15. *Do It! Let's Get Off Our Buts,* by Peter McWilliams and John-Roger. Prelude Press

1992

FICTION

1. *Dolores Claiborne,* by Stephen King. Viking Penguin

2. *The Pelican Brief,* by John Grisham. Doubleday

3. *Gerald's Game,* by Stephen King. Viking Penguin

4. *Mixed Blessings,* by Danielle Steel. Delacorte

5. *Jewels,* by Danielle Steel. Delacorte

6. *The Stars Shine Down,* by Sidney Sheldon. Morrow

7. *Tale of the Body Thief,* by Anne Rice. Knopf

8. *Mexico,* by James A. Michener. Random House

9. *Waiting to Exhale,* by Terry McMillan. Viking Penguin

10. *All Around the Town,* by Mary Higgins Clark. Simon & Schuster

11. *Scruples Two,* by Judith Krantz. Crown

12. *Sahara,* by Clive Cussler. Simon & Schuster

13. *Hideaway,* by Dean R. Koontz. Putnam

14. *The Road to Omaha,* by Robert Ludlum. Random House

15. *Star Wars: Dark Force Rising,* by Timothy Zahn. Bantam

Nonfiction

1. *The Way Things Ought to Be,* by Rush Limbaugh. Pocket Books

2. *It Doesn't Take a Hero: The Autobiography,* by General H. Norman Schwarzkopf. Bantam

3. *How to Satisfy a Woman Every Time,* by Naura Hayden. Bibli O' Phile

4. *Every Living Thing,* by James Herriot. St. Martin's

5. *A Return to Love,* by Marianne Williamson. HarperCollins

6. *Sam Walton: Made in America,* by Sam Walton. Doubleday

7. *Diana: Her True Story,* by Andrew Morton. Simon & Schuster

8. *Truman,* by David McCullough. Simon & Schuster

9. *Silent Passage,* by Gail Sheehy. Random House

10. *Sex,* by Madonna. Warner Books

11. *The Juiceman's Power of Juicing,* by Ray Kordich. Morrow

12. *Harvey Penick's Little Red Book,* by Harvey Penick. Simon & Schuster

13. *More Wealth Without Risk,* by Charles Givens. Simon & Schuster

14. *I Can't Believe I Said That,* by Kathie Lee Gifford. Pocket Books

15. *Creating Love,* by John Bradshaw. Bantam

1993

FICTION

1. *The Bridges of Madison County,* by Robert James Waller. Warner

2. *The Client,* by John Grisham. Doubleday

3. *Slow Waltz at Cedar Bend,* by Robert James Waller. Warner

4. *Without Remorse,* by Tom Clancy. Putnam

5. *Nightmares and Dreamscapes,* by Stephen King. Viking Penguin

6. *Vanished,* by Danielle Steel. Delacorte

7. *Lasher,* by Anne Rice. Knopf

8. *Pleading Guilty,* by Scott Turow. Farrar, Straus & Giroux

9. *Like Water for Chocolate,* by Laura Esquivel. Doubleday

10. *The Scorpio Illusion,* by Robert Ludlum. Bantam

11. *The Golden Mean,* by Nick Bantock. Chronicle Books

12. *I'll Be Seeing You,* by Mary Higgins Clark. Simon & Schuster

13. *A Dangerous Fortune,* by Ken Follett. Delacorte

14. *Mr. Murder,* by Dean Koontz. Putnam

15. *Gai-Jin,* by James Clavell. Delacorte

NONFICTION

1. *See I Told You So,* by Rush Limbaugh. Pocket Books

2. *Private Parts,* by Howard Stern. Simon & Schuster

3. *Seinlanguage,* by Jerry Seinfeld. Bantam

4. *Embraced By the Light,* by Betty J. Eadie with Curtis Taylor. Gold Leaf Press

5. *Ageless Body, Timeless Mind,* by Deepak Chopra. Harmony Books

6. *Stop the Insanity,* by Susan Powter. Simon & Schuster

7. *Women Who Run with the Wolves,* by Clarissa Pinkola Estes. Ballantine

8. *Men Are from Mars, Woman Are from Venus*, by John Gray. HarperCollins

9. *The Hidden Life of Dogs,* by Elizabeth Marshall Thomas. Houghton Mifflin

10. *And If You Play Golf, You're My Friend,* by Harvey Penick with Bud Shrake. Simon & Schuster

11. *The Way Things Ought to Be,* by Rush Limbaugh. Pocket Books

12. *Beating the Street,* by Peter Lynch with John Rothchild. Simon & Schuster

13. *Harvey Penick's Little Red Book,* by Harvey Penick with Bud Shrake. Simon & Schuster

14. *Wouldn't Take Nothing for My Journey Now,* by Maya Angelou. Random House

15. *Further Along the Road Less Traveled,* by M. Scott Peck, M. D. Simon & Schuster

1994

FICTION

1. *The Chamber,* by John Grisham. Doubleday

2. *Debt of Honor,* by Tom Clancy. Putnam

3. *The Celestine Prophecy,* by James Redfield. Warner

4. *The Gift,* by Danielle Steel. Delacorte

5. *Insomnia,* by Stephen King. Viking

6. *Politically Correct Bedtime Stories,* by James Finn Garner. Macmillan

7. *Wings,* by Danielle Steel. Delacorte

8. *Accident,* by Danielle Steel. Delacorte

9. *The Bridges of Madison County,* by Robert James Waller. Warner

10. *Disclosure,* by Michael Crichton. Knopf

11. *Nothing Lasts Forever,* by Sidney Sheldon. Morrow

12. *Taltos,* by Anne Rice. Knopf

13. *Dark Rivers of the Heart,* by Dean Koontz. Knopf

14. *The Lottery Winner,* by Mary Higgins Clark. Simon & Schuster

15. *Remember Me,* by Mary Higgins Clark. Simon & Schuster

NONFICTION

1. *In the Kitchen with Rosie,* by Rosie Daley. Knopf

2. *Men Are from Mars, Women Are from Venus,* by John Gray. HarperCollins

3. *Crossing the Threshold of Hope,* by John Paul II. Knopf

4. *Magic Eye I,* by N. E. Thing Enterprises. Andrews & McMeel

5. *The Book of Virtues,* ed. by William J. Bennett. Simon & Schuster

6. *Magic Eye II,* by N. E. Thing Enterprises. Andrews & McMeel

7. *Embraced by the Light,* by Betty J. Eadie with Curtis Taylor. Gold Leaf Press

8. *Don't Stand Too Close to a Naked Man,* by Tim Allen. Hyperion

9. *Couplehood,* by Paul Reiser. Bantam

10. *Magic Eye III,* by N. E. Thing Enterprises. Andrews & McMeel

11. *Dolly,* by Dolly Parton. HarperCollins

12. *James Herriot's Cat Stories,* by James Herriot. St. Martin's

13. *Barbara Bush,* by Barbara Bush. Scribner

14. *Nicole Brown Simpson,* by Faye D. Resnick. Dove Books

15. *The Bubba Gump Shrimp Co. Cookbook.* Oxmoor House/Leisure Arts

1995

FICTION

1. *The Rainmaker,* by John Grisham. Doubleday

2. *The Lost World,* by Michael Crichton. Knopf

3. *Five Days in Paris,* by Danielle Steel. Delacorte

4. *The Christmas Box,* by Richard Paul Evans. Simon & Schuster

5. *Lightning,* by Danielle Steel. Delacorte

6. *The Celestine Prophecy,* by James Redfield. Warner

7. *Rose Madder,* by Stephen King. Viking

8. *Silent Night,* by Mary Higgins Clark. Simon & Schuster

9. *Politically Correct Holiday Stories,* by James Finn Garner. Macmillan

10. *The Horse Whisperer,* by Nicholas Evans. Delacorte

11. *Politically Correct Bedtime Stories,* by James Finn Garner. Macmillan

12. *Memnoch the Devil,* by Anne Rice. Knopf

13. *Beach Music,* by Pat Conroy. Doubleday

14. *From Potter's Field,* by Patricia Cornwell. Scribner

15. *Morning, Noon and Night,* by Sidney Sheldon. Morrow

Nonfiction

1. *Men Are from Mars, Women Are from Venus,* by John Gray. HarperCollins

2. *My American Journey,* by Colin Powell with Joseph Persico. Random House

3. *Miss America,* by Howard Stern. ReganBooks

4. *The Seven Spiritual Laws of Success,* by Deepak Chopra. New World Library

5. *The Road Ahead,* by Bill Gates. Viking

6. *Charles Kuralt's America,* by Charles Kuralt. Putnam

7. *Mars and Venus in the Bedroom,* by John Gray. HarperCollins

8. *To Renew America,* by Newt Gingrich. HarperCollins

9. *My Point…and I Do Have One,* by Ellen DeGeneres. Bantam

10. *The Moral Compass,* by William J. Bennett. Simon & Schuster

11. *The Book of Virtues,* ed. by William J. Bennett. Simon & Schuster

12. *I Want to Tell You,* by O. J. Simpson with Laurence Schiller. Little, Brown

13. *In the Kitchen with Rosie,* by Rosie Daley. Knopf

14. *Emotional Intelligence,* by Daniel Goleman. Bantam

15. *David Letterman's Book of Top 10 Lists,* by David Letterman. Bantam

1996

FICTION

1. *The Runaway Jury,* by John Grisham. Doubleday

2. *Executive Orders,* by Tom Clancy. Putnam

3. *Desperation,* by Stephen King. Viking

4. *Airframe,* by Michael Crichton. Knopf

5. *The Regulators,* by Richard Bachman. Dutton

6. *Malice,* by Danielle Steel. Delacorte

7. *Silent Honor,* by Danielle Steel. Delacorte

8. *Primary Colors,* by Anonymous. Random House

9. *Cause of Death,* by Patricia Cornwell. Putnam

10. *The Tenth Insight,* by James Redfield. Warner

11. *The Deep End of the Ocean,* by Jacquelyn Mitchard. Viking

12. *How Stella Got Her Groove Back,* by Terry McMillan. Viking

13. *Moonlight Becomes You,* by Mary Higgins Clark. Simon & Schuster

14. *My Gal Sunday,* by Mary Higgins Clark. Simon & Schuster

15. *The Celestine Prophecy,* by James Redfield. Warner

Nonfiction

1. *Make the Connection,* by Oprah Winfrey and Bob Greene. Hyperion

2. *Men Are from Mars, Women Are from Venus,* by John Gray. HarperCollins

3. *The Dilbert Principle,* by Scott Adams. HarperBusiness

4. *Simple Abundance,* by Sarah Ban Breathnach. Warner

5. *The Zone,* by Barry Sears with Bill Lawren. ReganBooks

6. *Bad As I Wanna Be,* by Dennis Rodman. Delacorte

7. *In Contempt,* by Christopher Darden. ReganBooks

8. *A Reporter's Life,* by Walter Cronkite. Knopf

9. *Dogbert's Top Secret Management Handbook,* by Scott Adams. HarperBusiness

10. *My Sergei: A Love Story,* by Ekaterina Gordeeva with E. M. Swift. Warner

11. *Gift and Mystery,* by Pope John Paul II. Doubleday

12. *I'm Not Really Here,* by Tim Allen. Hyperion

13. *Rush Limbaugh Is a Big Fat Idiot and Other Observations,* by Al Franken. Delacorte

14. *James Herriot's Favorite Dog Stories,* by James Herriot. St. Martin's

15. *My Story,* by The Duchess of York. Simon & Schuster

1 9 9 7

FICTION

1. *The Partner,* by John Grisham. Doubleday

2. *Cold Mountain,* by Charles Frazier. Atlantic Monthly

3. *The Ghost,* by Danielle Steel. Delacorte

4. *The Ranch,* by Danielle Steel. Delacorte

5. *Special Delivery,* by Danielle Steel. Delacorte

6. *Unnatural Exposure,* by Patricia Cornwell. Putnam

7. *The Best Laid Plans,* by Sidney Sheldon. Morrow

8. *Pretend You Don't See Her,* by Mary Higgins Clark. Simon & Schuster

9. *Cat & Mouse,* by James Patterson. Little, Brown

10. *Hornet's Nest,* by Patricia Cornwell. Putnam

11. *The Letter,* by Richard Paul Evans. Simon & Schuster

12. *Flood Tide,* by Clive Cussler. Simon & Schuster

13. *Violin,* by Anne Rice. Knopf

14. *The Matarese Countdown,* by Robert Ludlum. Bantam

15. *Plum Island,* by Nelson DeMille. Warner

Nonfiction

1. *Angela's Ashes,* by Frank McCourt. Scribner

2. *Simple Abundance,* by Sarah Ban Breathnach. Warner

3. *Midnight in the Garden of Good and Evil,* by John Berendt. Random House

4. *The Royals,* by Kitty Kelley. Warner

5. *Joy of Cooking,* by Irma S. Rombauer, Marion Rombauer Becker and

   Ethan Becker. Scribner

6. *Diana: Her True Story,* by Andrew Morton. Simon & Schuster

7. *Into Thin Air,* by Jon Krakauer. Villard

8. *Conversations with God, Book I,* by Neale Donald Walsch. Putnam

9. *Men Are from Mars, Women Are from Venus,* by John Gray. HarperCollins

10. *Eight Weeks to Optimum Health,* by Andrew Weil. Knopf

11. *Just As I Am,* by Billy Graham. Harper San Francisco/Zondervan

12. *The Man Who Listens to Horses,* by Monty Roberts. Random House

13. *The Millionaire Next Door,* by Thomas J. Stanley and William D.

    Danko. Longstreet

14. *The Perfect Storm,* by Sebastian Junger. Norton

15. *Kids Are Punny,* by Rosie O'Donnell. Warner

1998

FICTION

1. *The Street Lawyer,* by John Grisham. Doubleday

2. *Rainbow Six,* by Tom Clancy. Putnam

3. *Bag of Bones,* by Stephen King. Scribner

4. *A Man in Full,* by Tom Wolfe. Farrar, Straus & Giroux

5. *Mirror Image,* by Danielle Steel. Delacorte

6. *The Long Road Home,* by Danielle Steel. Delacorte

7. *The Klone and I,* by Danielle Steel. Delacorte

8. *Point of Origin,* by Patricia Cornwell. Putnam

9. *Paradise,* by Toni Morrison. Knopf

10. *All Through the Night,* by Mary Higgins Clark. Simon & Schuster

11. *I Know This Much Is True,* by Wally Lamb. HarperCollins/ReganBooks

12. *Tell Me Your Dreams,* by Sidney Sheldon. Morrow

13. *The Vampire Armand,* by Anne Rice. Knopf

14. *The Loop,* by Nicholas Evans. Delacorte

15. *You Belong to Me,* by Mary Higgins Clark. Simon & Schuster

NONFICTION

1. *The 9 Steps to Financial Freedom,* by Suze Orman. Crown

2. *The Greatest Generation,* by Tom Brokaw. Random House

3. *Sugar Busters!* by H. Leighton Steward, Morrison C. Bethea, Sam S. Andrews and Luis A. Balart. Ballantine

4. *Tuesdays with Morrie,* by Mitch Albom. Doubleday

5. *The Guinness Book of Records 1999.* Guinness Media

6. *Talking to Heaven,* by James Van Praagh. Dutton

7. *Something More: Excavating Your Authentic Self,* by Sarah Ban Breathnach. Warner

8. *In the Meantime,* by Iyanla Vanzant. Simon & Schuster

9. *A Pirate Looks at Fifty,* by Jimmy Buffett. Random House

10. *If Life Is a Game These Are the Rules,* by Cherie Carter-Scott, Ph. D. Broadway Books

11. *Angela's Ashes,* by Frank McCourt. Scribner

12. *For the Love of the Game: My Story,* by Michael Jordan. Crown

13. *The Day Diana Died,* by Christopher Andersen. Morrow

14. *The Century,* by Peter Jennings and Todd Brewster. Doubleday

15. *Eat Right 4 Your Type,* by Peter J. D'Adamo. Putnam

1999

FICTION

1. *The Testament,* by John Grisham. Doubleday

2. *Hannibal,* by Thomas Harris. Delacorte

3. *Assassins,* by Jerry B. Jenkins and Tim LaHaye. Tyndale

4. *Star Wars: Episode 1, The Phantom Menace,* by Terry Brooks. Lucas Books/Del Rey

5. *Timeline,* by Michael Crichton. Knopf

6. *Hearts in Atlantis,* by Stephen King. Scribner

7. *Apollyon,* by Jerry B. Jenkins and Tim LaHaye. Tyndale

8. *The Girl Who Loved Tom Gordon,* by Stephen King. Scribner

9. *Irresistible Forces,* by Danielle Steel. Delacorte

10. *Tara Road,* by Maeve Binchy. Delacorte

11. *White Oleander,* by Janet Fitch. Little, Brown

12. *A Walk to Remember,* by Nicholas Sparks. Warner

13. *Pop Goes the Weasel,* by James Patterson. Little, Brown

14. *Black Notice,* by Patricia Cornwell. Putnam

15. *Granny Dan,* by Danielle Steel. Delacorte

NONFICTION

1. *Tuesdays with Morrie,* by Mitch Albom. Doubleday

2. *The Greatest Generation,* by Tom Brokaw. Random House

3. *Guinness World Records 2000 Millennium Edition.* Guinness Publishing

4. *'Tis,* by Frank McCourt. Scribner

5. *Who Moved My Cheese?* by Spencer Johnson. Putnam

6. *The Courage to Be Rich,* by Suze Orman. Riverhead

7. *The Greatest Generation Speaks,* by Tom Brokaw. Random House

8. *Sugar Busters!* by H. Leighton Steward, Morrison C. Bethea, Sam S. Andrews and Luis A. Balart. Ballantine

9. *The Art of Happiness,* by the Dalai Lama and Howard C. Cutler. Riverhead

10. *The Century,* by Peter Jennings and Todd Brewster. Doubleday

11. *Body for Life,* by Bill Phillips. HarperCollins

12. *Life Strategies,* by Phillip C. McGraw. Hyperion

13. *Have a Nice Day!* by Mick Foley. ReganBooks

14. *Suzanne Somers' Get Skinny on Fabulous Food,* by Suzanne Somers. Crown

15. *Don't Sweat the Small Stuff in Love,* by Richard and Kristine Carlson. Hyperion

EPILOGUE

❧

I N B O O K S , A S I N O T H E R T H I N G S, there is nothing new under
the sun. What people read changes in style, like what they wear; still
clothes are clothes, however fashionable. In book publishing, trends have
always been cyclical, from the very beginning of the list. For example, while
there have been periods in which "sexy" novels made their way onto the list—
think back to *Forever Amber,* then the period of Jacqueline Susann's bestsellers—most of the novels on the 1999 list could have been published in
1895 without raising an eyebrow or upsetting the authorities in Boston,
except for Thomas Harris's *Hannibal,* and that not because it was overtly sexy,
but because of its theme of cannibalism and eroticism. The sexy novel seems
to have gone altogether out of fashion (for how long, one wonders?). After a
long period in which the ability to write a sex scene was considered the *ne
plus ultra* of bestseller writing, it seems to have vanished off the lists—Harold
Robbins, Irving Wallace, Erica Jong, and countless others once competed to
write sex scenes, most of which would raise nothing but a yawn today, and
novelists who coveted a place on the list were often advised to begin the novel

"with a bang," the general opinion being that if you gave the reader a big, shocking sex scene on page one, he or she would certainly keep reading the next few hundred pages in pursuit of another. Readers, however, grew bored with sex as quickly as they grow bored with anything else—maybe quicker, in fact—and most of the big bestsellers these days make Gene Stratton Porter's *Girl of the Limberlost* look sexy. Many of the biggest bestsellers, like those of Tom Clancy, have no sex in them at all—if there's any pornographic content in Clancy, it's the pornography of violence and weaponry. Probably the simple truth is that "adult" channels on cable television and the "triple-X-rated" videocassette brought real, filmed sex into the home for those who wanted it, and made reading about it in books seem old-fashioned. What really mattered in fiction, it turned out, not surprisingly, was story, not sex.

If the sexy novel has vanished, the tearjerker has not (*The Bridges of Madison County* was a classic tearjerker, with one mildly sexual scene thrown in, true, but otherwise very much in the tradition of Gene Stratton Porter). As for historical fiction, certainly Michael Crichton's *Timeline* would have been at home on the 1895 list, since it follows in the tradition of Mark Twain's classic *A Connecticut Yankee in King Arthur's Court*. In general, historical novels don't change much over the decades. What look like big, original leaps forward turn out to be, in fact, only small ones. Jean M. Auel, for example, writes what are essentially romantic historical novels set in prehistory, but the formula isn't that different from any other big historical drama with a heroine at the center. It's just that the period is more remote—bearskins and raw mammoth meat instead of crinolines and juleps on the porch, or mobcaps and "The redcoats are coming!"

As for nonfiction, how different is the list today from what Americans were reading a hundred years ago? Not very, is the answer. Celebrities, political history and scandal, self-help and cookbooks brought Americans into the bookstore then, as now, and what seems most new is usually just a gloss on the old.

Of course the real excitement in book publishing in the nineties wasn't the books, or even the mergers that seemed likely to end in their being only one big bookstore chain and one universal publishing house, but the advent of the "e-book," and with it the possibility that the book itself was dead, a technological blind alley, to be replaced by the digital delivery of "content," as the corporate owners of publishing houses now liked to call books, possibly direct to the home.

Stephen King, ever the pioneer—with *The Green Mile,* he reinvented the old Victorian tradition of publishing a novel in parts—was the first to publish an electronic book, available on the Internet, at first in cooperation with his publisher, then on his own, in competition with his publisher. The results are hard to assess. The book as an article of commerce, in its present form, seems likely to be with us for some time, and with it, the book publisher and the bookseller, but it is possible that the future of books will eventually be electronic—that paper, perhaps, will have had its day, as did the papyrus scroll and before that the baked clay tablet.

The invention of printing—and of the book—was one of the great technological revolutions, and had far-reaching effects on mankind: the spread of knowledge in an easily portable form brought about, at any rate in Europe and eventually America, the end of the Universal Church, the Enlightenment, the political transformations that would culminate in the American and the French Revolutions, and much else besides, but that is not to say that the book is any more sacred and permanent as a means of storing culture, entertainment, information, and knowledge than its predecessors. A day is surely coming when it will be possible to summon up any book that has ever been published on the Internet, and print it out in some convenient way at home, and when there will be, as a result, no such thing as an "out-of-print" title, or even one that is "out-of-stock." Writers will display their books and offer sample chapters of them on their Web sites, changing the roles of agent and publisher, perhaps even one day eliminating the latter, at any rate.

On the other hand, perhaps not. Some mechanism will still be needed to publicize and market the book, not to speak of editing it, and some mechanism will be needed to sell it, so in some form or other the bookstore and the book publisher (and the agent) will continue to do what they have always done, albeit, perhaps, in a different form.

One thing is certain: Even if everything changes and the whole process of publishing becomes digital—a change that, in my opinion, is going to take very much longer than anybody supposes, and will always contain a place for people who still want to shop for books and to read them the old-fashioned way—there will still be a bestseller list, recording which titles are getting the most "hits," and somebody is still going to be "#1."

In the meantime, the list goes on, as it has for 107 years, defining, from week to week, what it is that Americans are reading, in whatever form it comes to them.

Like a mirror, it reflects who we are, what we want, what interests us, and what we really want to know, and our peculiarly American combination of a thirst for adventure and a yearning for enlightenment, the Puritan urge to improve our minds and the equally characteristic desire to kick up our heels and have a good time, and the longer we look into it, the more we clearly see—*ourselves*.

INDEX

(does not include citations to the actual bestseller lists)